Integrating M...
Students int...
Classrooms

MIX
Paper from
responsible sources

FSC
www.fsc.org **FSC® C014540**

Full details of all our books can be found on http://www.multilingual-matters.com, or by writing to Multilingual Matters, St Nicholas House, 31–34 High Street, Bristol, BS1 2AW, UK.

Integrating Multilingual Students into College Classrooms

Practical Advice for Faculty

Johnnie Johnson Hafernik and Fredel M. Wiant

MULTILINGUAL MATTERS
Bristol • Buffalo • Toronto

To our colleagues and our students

Library of Congress Cataloging in Publication Data
A catalog record for this book is available from the Library of Congress.
Hafernik, Johnnie Johnson.
Integrating Multilingual Students into College Classrooms: Practical Advice for Faculty/
Johnnie Johnson Hafernik and Fredel M. Wiant.
Includes bibliographical references and index.
1. English language--Study and teaching (Higher)--Foreign speakers. 2. Academic language--Study and teaching. 3. Multilingualism. I. Wiant, Fredel M. II. Title.
PE1128.A2H283 2012
428.0071'173–dc23 2012022014

British Library Cataloguing in Publication Data
A catalogue entry for this book is available from the British Library.

ISBN-13: 978-1-84769-820-9 (hbk)
ISBN-13: 978-1-84769-819-3 (pbk)

Multilingual Matters
UK: St Nicholas House, 31-34 High Street, Bristol, BS1 2AW, UK.
USA: UTP, 2250 Military Road, Tonawanda, NY 14150, USA.
Canada: UTP, 5201 Dufferin Street, North York, Ontario, M3H 5T8, Canada.

Channel View Publications
UK: St Nicholas House, 31-34 High Street, Bristol BS1 2AW, UK.
USA: UTP, 2250 Military Road, Tonawanda, NY 14150, USA.
Canada: UTP, 5201 Dufferin Street, North York, Ontario M3H 5T8, Canada.

The policy of Multilingual Matters/Channel View Publications is to use papers that are natural, renewable and recyclable products, made from wood grown in sustainable forests. In the manufacturing process of our books, and to further support our policy, preference is given to printers that have FSC and PEFC Chain of Custody certification. The FSC and/or PEFC logos will appear on those books where full certification has been granted to the printer concerned.

Typeset by The Charlesworth Group.
Printed and bound in Great Britain by Short Run Press Ltd.

Contents

Acknowledgments

We are indebted to many individuals for assistance, encouragement and support throughout the process of writing this book. First, we thank several administrators at the University of San Francisco who create an atmosphere where writing, research and other scholarly endeavors are encouraged and appreciated and where diversity, in its broadest definition, is promoted and valued. The Dean's office in the College of Arts and Sciences has long supported weekly writing groups and weekend writing retreats, which have provided structure and community for our writing. For their interest and support of our work, we thank the members of these writing communities and Pamela Balls Organista, organizer of the writing retreats, and Tracy Seeley, organizer of the on-campus writing groups. In the Dean's office for the College of Arts and Sciences, we thank Dean Marcelo Camperi, Associate Dean Eileen Fung and former Associate Dean Peter Novak, now Vice Provost of Student Life. We owe a special thanks to Provost and Vice President for Academic Affairs, Jennifer Turpin, who was Dean of the College of Arts and Sciences when we began this project and who oversaw the formation of our department, the Department of Rhetoric and Language.

Numerous faculty and students generously allowed us to interview them, giving us thoughtful and insightful comments about their experiences, challenges and values. We are grateful for their contributions. We thank Fred Baldwin and Alan Ziajika for helping us gather statistics. We thank Marc Martin, Christy Newman and Cynthia Schultes for sharing their grading rubrics. We have benefited from formal and informal conversations with colleagues and friends within the Department of Rhetoric and Language, across the university and in the larger academic community. In particular, we are indebted to Dennis Bacigalupi, Mark Meritt and Constance O'Keefe for lively discussions and unique perspectives. Bernadette Pedagno read the manuscript, providing us invaluable feedback and suggestions, for which we are most appreciative. We owe a special debt of gratitude to our colleague Stephanie Vandrick for her generosity, critiques of early drafts, encouragement and unwavering belief in us and the project.

We also thank two anonymous reviewers for Multilingual Matters whose thoughtful and extensive comments helped us rethink and revise our manuscript in ways that have strengthened the book. We thank our editors

Tommi Grover and Anna Roderick for their interest and guidance through-out the process and the production team members, Laura Longworth and Sarah Williams, for their assistance. Finally, J.J.H. is grateful for the patience, insights into academic life and loving support of her husband, John E. Hafernik, and daughter, Carolyn Theresa Hafernik.

Introduction

The work is waiting for us. And so irrevocable now is the tide that brings the new students into the nation's college classrooms that it is no longer within our power, as perhaps it once was, to refuse to accept them into the community of the educable. They are here.
Mina Shaughnessy (1998: 7)

The students of whom Shaughnessy writes are *our* students – the international, the first generation and other multilingual students who increasingly compose a portion of our student bodies and many of whom often get lumped together as remedial. In this book, we will argue that these students are not all the same: they are not all basic writers, readers and speakers, and to label multilingual students as such is not only a disservice to them but often prevents us from seeing the insights they can offer, the subject matter knowledge they have mastered and their potential as resources to us, their peers and our institutions. We will argue, as Shaughnessy (1998) does, that we need to muster 'professional courage – the decision to remediate [our]selves, to become student[s] of new disciplines and of [our] students themselves in order to perceive both their difficulties and their incipient excellence' (Shaughnessy, 1998: 7). Shaughnessy was, of course, addressing the issue of basic writers; today we confront a larger, more diverse group of students and in this book we do not limit ourselves to discussing students only as writers, but as complex individuals who are members of the academic community and who must exercise the full range of academic skills – reading, writing, speaking and listening. Nonetheless, her admonition is still evocative of the challenges we face.

Specifically, we must reject the assumption that the 'norm' on university campuses today is, or should be, the monolingual English speaker – the attitude that Roberge (2009: 5) labels as 'nativist normality'. No longer is the monocultural, monolingual English speaker the 'average' or 'normal' student (Canagarajah, 2006: 216). A new vision of, and new strategies for, integrating multilingual students into the academy must emerge. A goal of this book is to imagine such a vision and outline strategies for moving toward it.

In an odd way, our book began with a newly renovated building. For years the ESL program and the Program in Rhetoric and Composition at our university, though part of the same larger department, were housed in separate buildings some two blocks apart. Many of the faculty members did not

1

even know each other. In the fall of 2008, however, renovation was completed on an historic campus building that allowed the programs to have shared office space. From that rose a new level of collaboration. Not only did our faculties meet each other, but also we began to work together. Out of that spirit of collaboration we were able to identify and discuss some of the problems that confronted our faculty and our students and to devise strategies to address them; eventually we merged into our own department. We take this as a lesson: whenever possible, even if there is not a common space, creating community will enhance both scholarship and teaching, bringing rewards to both students and faculty.

The creation of this cohesive department and community enabled better communication, revealing common areas of interest and concern. Because we became more identifiable as the place to go for resources on literacy and communication skills, and because of increasing numbers of multilingual speakers enrolling in our institution, we began to hear more and more concerns from faculty in other departments and schools about the English facility of students in their classes. Finding no small, accessible guidebook to recommend to faculty we decided to write one. This book is designed for our colleagues across the disciplines who find multilingual students in their classes, colleagues who strive to help each student succeed but are often unsure how to assist them.

We should note that the United States is not the only nation with a significant number of international students – Australia, Canada, France, Germany and the United Kingdom also enroll large numbers of students from abroad. In fact, these countries 'hosted more than half of the world's students who studied abroad in 2009' (GlobalHigherEd, 2011: 3). Therefore, we believe this book will be helpful to faculties in those countries as well.

We bring to this enterprise scholarly work, and years of teaching, in three disciplines: TESOL and Linguistics (Hafernik), Rhetoric and Composition and Communication (Wiant). We have, in those years, encountered, like you, a large number of students, both mono- and multilingual, in our classes and have observed their strengths as well as the difficulties they often encounter. Beyond that, together we have served at different times as Program Coordinators and Department Chairs of English as a Second Language, Rhetoric and Composition, Communication Studies, and a new Department of Rhetoric and Language that combines our two disciplines into one department that offers courses in English for Academic Purposes (EAP), Rhetoric and Composition and Public Speaking. In these administrative roles we have answered, more times than we can count, the questions from faculty that form the foundation of this book. We have conducted interviews with multilingual students and with faculty about challenges they face, have heard stories from colleagues in a variety of disciplines about working with diverse students, and have fielded questions from faculty about how best to assist students.

In working together, we have come to some common understandings about our approach to multilingual students in our classrooms and our universities. These understandings have shaped the book and provide a snapshot of our educational philosophies. First, multilingualism is positive and should be encouraged. Diversity on our campuses and in our classrooms is an asset – everyone gains. Many multilingual students are equally comfortable and proficient with English and one, two or more languages in daily and academic environments. These students seem to adjust to the use of English in the university with minimal difficulty and are generally welcomed. However, other multilingual students lack outward signs of having facility in academic English or of having learned traditional academic norms and behaviors. Although these students continue to improve their English and to become socialized to the academic community once they arrive on our campuses, they may be viewed less favorably than others and may even cause discomfort to some members of the academic community.

Second, limited English proficiency and limited awareness of academic norms do not mean limited intelligence or limited academic ability. Many of our students with emerging English are extremely bright, well-read in their native language and excellent critical thinkers. They have much to contribute to academic communities. Given sufficient support in mastering the language and navigating the college environment, they may well become some of our most outstanding students.

The students we speak of display some English proficiency. We assume that all of them have studied English elsewhere, either in their high schools, an EFL or ESL course in their home countries or a language institute either here or abroad. We also assume that they have met the admission requirements of the institution they attend.

Third, 'compartmentalizing' courses (e.g. providing different courses or sections for multilingual students and for native English speakers) (Valdés, 2006) or marginalizing our students is counterproductive for all members of the academy. Everyone benefits when multilingual students are 'mainstreamed' in all classes including composition and public speaking, although multilingual students may initially benefit from being given the option of enrolling in a section of these courses with a TESOL-trained instructor. In such classroom environments, they may feel more comfortable and take more linguistic risks, leading to more rapid improvement in their linguistic skills. Students, however, should be able to self-select into such sections and not be required to take them. In our experience, most students prefer the mainstreamed sections because they inherently understand that being in classes with those whose English is fluent will help them improve their language skills and because most want to receive the same education as other students. If they need additional support, many, if not most, campuses have learning, writing and/or speaking centers available that can provide multilingual students with resources.

Fourth, labels such as 'remedial' or 'developmental', to describe multilingual speakers who are working on their English proficiency, are seductive and misleading. Both terms suggest an affinity for the 'deficit model' (Canagarajah, 2006; Rose, 1985; Zamel, 1994) of language and learning in which the emphasis is placed on what the students *don't* know rather than what they *do* know. We need a new vocabulary that appreciates diversity, one that highlights the positive. Others suggest a 'difference model' whereas Canagarajah (2006) argues for a 'resource model' as a more positive image; we prefer the term 'possibility model'.

Finally, all faculty can and should assist multilingual students in improving their academic English proficiency and their knowledge of 'how to' be a scholar. These tasks cannot be limited to those who teach English as a Second Language, composition or speech communication. Studies (e.g. Johns, 1991) have shown that all students, including English Language Learners, continue to gain proficiency in English skills throughout their academic and professional careers. In fact, individuals never stop learning.

The argument that all faculty can assist students in improving their linguistic and academic skills does not mean, however, that faculty need to 'teach English' or teach reading, speaking or writing. Faculty focus on content in their disciplines, whether that is computer science, physics, theology or literature; in fact, they often feel there is insufficient time to cover everything that is necessary. However, at the same time that faculty are assisting students in the learning of content, they can assist students in improving their English and in learning the ways of academe. Our goal in this book is to offer practical advice for faculty in doing just that.

This book is not a manual that will miraculously turn all faculty into ESL specialists. We do not pretend to know all the answers or to solve all the problems; we are not even certain that we have addressed all the questions that faculty may have. Our goal is to help students and faculty be strategic about learning by sharing some observations and strategies that can be applied across the curriculum.

A Note to Our Readers

Now that we have affirmed what this book is *not,* we turn to what the book *is*. This is a book designed to offer assistance for faculty across the disciplines. It contains two parts: Part 1: The Context and Part 2: Understanding and Addressing Language Skills. The first task in understanding the context of today's university is getting to know the students. We do this in Chapter 1: Our Students by describing multilingual students (including those commonly called 'Generation 1.5') demographically and culturally and by paying special attention to the similarities and differences between multilingual students and native speakers. We also address various learning styles and classroom practices that may be distinguishing features of students from other cultures. We conclude the first chapter by addressing some of the common 'myths' or misperceptions that we have encountered from faculty and students about the role of multilingual students on our campuses. In Chapter 2: Constructing Classrooms Where Students Can Succeed, we briefly explain four fundamental aspects of second and additional language acquisition and present six guidelines for building inclusive classrooms.

Part 2: Understanding and Addressing Language Skills contains an introduction and six chapters. In the Introduction, we explain the types of knowledge that students need for academic success. In each of the next four chapters, we focus on one of the four basic language skills – speaking, listening, reading and writing – outlining common academic tasks for each and offering practical advice for helping students successfully accomplish these academic tasks. In Chapter 7: Working in Groups, we focus on the why, how and when of structuring and assigning group projects and offer suggestions for making group work an effective learning activity. In Chapter 8: Assessment, we explore what assessing student work entails and include answers to a list of frequently asked questions we have heard from colleagues in a variety of disciplines. The book ends with an epilogue that moves from the university to a larger context.

Throughout the book, we have strived to be gender neutral. In that effort, we have used plural pronouns whenever possible. When singular pronouns are appropriate, we have used male singular pronouns in the introduction to the book and the odd numbered chapters (one, three, five, seven and nine), and we have used female singular pronouns in the Introduction to Part 2, even numbered chapters (e.g. two, four, six and eight), the epilogue and the glossary.

As much as we hope faculty will read the entire book, the chapters, and even sections within chapters, are independent. We have sought to make the book reader-friendly and enjoyable reading for faculty in all disciplines. We hope that faculty will turn to it as a quick reference to resolve a particular question or issue, as well as to gain a better understanding of their multilingual students. We offer suggestions and advice not as definitive answers, but as a springboard for faculty to reflect upon their own students and teaching contexts and to develop strategies for helping all students achieve success in academe. We hope you find our book useful.

Part 1

The Context

1 Our Students

> *In order to break down compartments now existing within the profession, [we] must*
> *begin to see the 'new' student population not as a special group destined to disappear*
> *quickly into the mainstream but as a population that will significantly change the character*
> *of the entire student community in this country. Tomorrow's mainstream student group will*
> *be made up of what we consider today to be 'diverse' students.*
> Guadalupe Valdés (2006: 64–65)

There are, as of the time of writing, 723,277 international students enrolled in United States colleges and universities (Institute of International Education, 2011). This does not include students who are US citizens or permanent residents and whose native language is not English, nor does it include students who may speak one language at home and a second language at school. These students are described by a number of labels and served by a veritable alphabet soup of programs. We realize that categorizing students, however it is done, is at least problematic, if not controversial. We do not wish to essentialize students and seek instead to recognize each as an individual. Nonetheless, certain categories can be helpful in understanding the distinctive linguistic and cultural issues that arise among our students.

Demographics of Multilingual Students

International students

As we noted above, there are currently over 700,000 students who are classified as international students – those who are studying here on student visas and intend to return to their country of origin when their studies are completed – currently enrolled in US educational institutions, including community colleges and technical schools. This represents 3.5% of total college enrollment in the US (Institute of International Education, 2011). Roughly half are undergraduates and half are graduate students, with a much smaller number of non-degree seeking students. The Institute of International Education (IIE), which conducts an annual census of international students in the US, notes that of these, approximately half come from just five countries – China, India, South Korea, Canada and Taiwan. Of particular note is the significant increase in the number of students reporting China as their country of origin – a 29.8% increase in the one-year period 2008/9 to 2009/10 (IIE, 2010) and a 23.5% increase from 2009/2010 to 2010/2011 (IIE, 2011). Duke University reported that the number of matriculated students from China increased in three years from 8% to 30%, and Carleton College reported that 'In the past few years, the number of annual applications from China has grown to 300 from 50 or 60 most years' (Jaschik, 2009). In 2010/2011, the country with the greatest increase over the previous year was Saudi Arabia (43.6%) (IIE, 2010). At the same time, there has been a significant decline (-14.3% in 2010/2011) in the number of Japanese students studying in the US (IIE, 2011).

Other countries that show a large number of international students include Germany and France (20%), Japan, Canada and New Zealand (13%), and Malaysia, Singapore and China (12%) (IIE, 2010). While each of the countries defines international student somewhat differently, the common factor is that the student is not a citizen and has traveled to that country with the express purpose of gaining an education. All these statistics highlight the fact that students on campuses in many countries are becoming more diverse, with increasing numbers of international students.

'Parachute kids'

A subset of international students are those who have attended high school, and sometimes middle school, at a boarding school in the US or another English-speaking country. These students are sometimes called 'parachute kids' in that they have been dropped or 'parachuted' into the educational boarding school system so that they do not live with their families on a full-time basis. Like all international students, they study on student visas and are not permanent residents. Often, after completing high school, they continue their education in the US. These students have often studied English in their native countries before coming to the US, but the English instruction may have been uneven and/or sporadic. In addition, those who attended boarding schools with large numbers of international students may have had little opportunity to interact with native English speakers. International students who graduate from US high schools generally take the SAT or ACT test rather than a TOEFL, IELTS or other standardized English test to gain admission to a US postsecondary institution.

Standardized tests, however, may be poor indicators of these students' English abilities because the students may be conversationally proficient in English but weak in academic English skills. Typically they do better on the math portions of standardized tests such as the SAT and ACT than the verbal sections. They may share some characteristics with native speakers in that they have absorbed American culture from movies, music, television, fashion or other influences, so they are often Americanized, yet they lack the academic skills needed to do college-level reading, writing, listening or even speaking. These students often escape our notice because of their apparent fluency, leaving us to wonder why they are having so much difficulty in the classroom.

Generation 1.5 students

The demographic data for international students does not account for all the multilingual students that may be in our classrooms. There are a number of other categories into which our students may fall, including a number of categories that pertain to US multilingual students. One significant and growing subset of multilingual students is that group generally referred to as Generation 1.5 (Gen 1.5), often a label of convenience. Defining these students and their backgrounds is difficult, as Harklau *et al.* (1999) and many others have noted. Harklau *et al.* (1999: 4–5) argue that definitions based on single characteristics are problematic. Common definitions include (a) a generational or resident status definition (when did they and/ or their parents arrive in the US); (b) an educational experience definition (how many years of US education have they had and was their schooling interrupted); or (c) an affiliational definition (what do they identify as their native language). Harklau and her co-authors conclude 'In all, the picture that emerges . . . is of a tremendously diverse student population along continua of language proficiency, language affiliation, and academic literacy backgrounds' (Harklau *et al.*, 1999: 5). Nonetheless, a typical feature of these students is that they speak their parents' native language in the home but English at school and with their friends. They may serve as translators both of language and culture for their parents and grandparents. Often they are the links between the native language and culture of their family and their family's adopted language and culture. Not surprisingly then, many consider themselves to be native English speakers or bilingual. They may have a feeling of 'between-ness', falling between the first and second generation immigrants. However, Matsuda and Matsuda (2009: 60) caution that 'the use of the term "generation 1.5" then is best understood as metaphorically – it is not to be taken too literally'.

Because many Gen 1.5 students identify themselves as native speakers of English, and because information about students' home languages and language abilities is not kept by K-12 or postsecondary institutions, the demographic figures for Gen 1.5 students are more difficult to obtain than figures for international students. Additionally, census figures do not count those of student age as a separate category. However, the 2007 US Census reported that there are 322 separate languages spoken by US residents (Shin & Bruno, 2003: 4). Over 55 million respondents said that they spoke a language other than English in the home. Of those, about 40 million indicated they spoke English 'well' or 'very well'; the rest chose 'not well' or 'not at all'. The predominant languages were Spanish (34.5 million), other Indo-European languages (10.3 million), Asian and Pacific Island languages (8.3 million) and Other (2.2 million) (Shin & Kominski, 2010: 2). Even though Gen 1.5 students indicate they speak a language other than English at home, they may use English extensively to communicate outside the family. Gen 1.5 students may not be completely fluent or literate in the language used in the home (variously called the Mother Tongue, Heritage Language, Home Language, First Language or Native Language), having been educated mostly in US schools. Harklau *et al.* (1999) note that although they speak English at school, their academic skills may be weak. They often do not self-identify with either international students or native English speakers, another instance of feeling 'inbetween-ness'. Many Gen 1.5 students have had interrupted educations due to their family situations and may have had no ESL instruction from qualified ESL instructors.

Blurring the Lines

The task of describing or labeling multilingual students is further complicated by the fact that regardless of which of the above groups they belong to, they are at different stages of their grasp of the second (or third or fourth) languages and each individual is unique. Diebold (1961: 99) coined the term *incipient bilingualism* to denote students who are beginning to learn the language, whereas *functional bilingualism* applies to those who are able to perform meaningful, but not necessarily grammatically accurate, communications.

A more recent essay (Valdés, 2006: 37) uses the terms *incipient* and *functional* with the same basic meanings as Diebold's, but further divides bi- or multilinguals into *elective* ('those who choose to become bilingual') versus *circumstantial* ('individuals who, because of their circumstances, find that they must learn another language in order to survive'). A simple example will illustrate the difference: a US native English speaker who chooses to study Spanish and becomes fluent is an elective bilingual; a worker who emigrates to the US from Mexico and must learn English to get a job is a circumstantial bilingual.

Cook (2002), on the other hand, rejects the designation of bilingual or multilingual and argues for the use of the term *L2 (second language) user*. In this case, an *L2 user* is defined as an individual who has knowledge of and facility with the language, as distinguished from an *L2 learner*, an individual who is still acquiring the L2. The differences in the terms is one of perception, with an L2 user viewed positively (he is capable of using the language) whereas an L2 learner is seen as less positive or even negative (he is somehow lacking in language skills). Drawing on research on monolinguals and multilinguals, Cook (2002: 9) emphasizes that 'the minds, languages, and lives of L2 users are different from those of monolinguals'. Valdés *et al.* (2009) cite both Cook and Grosjean in arguing that L2 users are not simply equivalent to two monolinguals. Rather they have, Valdés *et al.* (2009: 20) assert, 'acquired their two languages in particular contexts and for particular purposes'. The authors continue, 'By definition, L2 users have internalized two implicit linguistic knowledge systems – one in each of their languages.' In describing bilingualism, García (2009: 71) asserts that 'Bilingualism is not monolingualism times two'.

We struggle with the complexity of these multiple definitions and classifications and accept their inherent ambiguities. Just as we all belong to multiple groups and play multiple roles, so do our students. Complicating clear definitions and classifications is the complexity and variety within each group and the fluidity between groups. We continually must guard against placing students into strict categories and must strive to see them as unique individuals. Roberge (2009: 19) notes that any labels are problematic, whether they are *'Ethnic labels* that equate immigrants with US born minorities ... *Linguistic labels* such as "ESL" ... or *Academic labels* such as "remedial" or "basic writer"'. Nevertheless, for convenience sake, we must choose a term that, while admittedly inadequate in capturing the complexities, will provide a convenient 'handle' for the array of groups and categories. In this volume, we use the term *multilingual* to include all of these various categories: international students, including 'parachute kids', and Gen 1.5 students.

Multilinguals and Native Speakers: Much the Same but with a Difference

Although multilingual students are a diverse group culturally, linguistically and geographically, they share certain similarities among themselves and with native speakers. First and foremost, most want to succeed academically. In fact, in a recent poll (2012) of Chinese high school students who want to study in the United States, respondents listed a desire to 'learn

skills of critical thinking, problem solving, and intellectual creativity important to success in all fields today' as the single most important reason for
their interest in studying in the US, followed closely by their perception
that 'the US has the best colleges and universities in the world' (StudentPoll,
2012: 7). Beyond wanting to succeed academically, though, they share many
other interests and characteristics with all college students around the
world. New students may be apprehensive about the college experience and
unsure of their ability to succeed. The same poll of Chinese high school
students indicates that for these students, the most important concern,
reported by 45% of respondents, is whether they are 'academically prepared
to study in the US'. Another 28% are concerned about their English competency (StudentPoll, 2012: 8). Multilingual students want to make new
friends; they are concerned about social relationships; they generally enjoy
many of the same recreational activities – music, shopping, video games,
movies, sports; they get stressed about assignments and exams. They may
be adjusting to a new environment and living arrangement; they may suffer
from culture shock. As an example of concerns about adjusting to college
life, students in the StudentPoll China (StudentPoll, 2012: 8) reported that
they were concerned about their lack of knowledge of US schools (37%) and
about being such a distance from home (25%) and having difficulty leaving
their families (11%). Finally, after graduation they want a good job and to
lead a 'good life'. In other words, they are normal college students with all
the doubts, fears and hopes that are universal.

It should also be said, however, that, similar to native speakers, most of
our multilingual students are young people, and that means some of them
may exhibit the same unproductive habits as their native-speaking counter-
parts – missing class, not turning in assignments, not reading the required
materials. In these cases, multilingual students should be treated no differently than domestic students, and should understand that class rules apply
to them as well.

Like increasing numbers of college students overall, multilinguals have
mental health issues (e.g. homesickness, depression, substance abuse, eating
disorders, bipolar disorder) (Kadison & DiGeronimo, 2004; Soet & Sevig,
2006). Students may arrive on campuses with mental health issues or may
develop them upon arrival. Similarly, college is stressful for all students,
and multilingual students may have more stress associated with cultural
adjustment (i.e. culture shock), lack of support systems and new freedoms
than US students who are more familiar with US society and the academic
environment. Additionally, students deal with stress differently, and some
of this difference is cultural. Mori (2000) notes that US students tend
to experience stress as anxiety, depression or both, whereas international

students exhibit physical signs of stress and may not distinguish 'emotional distress' from 'physical distress'.

What do we as faculty do if we notice students exhibiting symptoms of stress or showing signs of violent or self-destructive behavior? First, we need to be mindful of the fact that cultural views of mental illness differ in terms of what constitute mental illnesses, how they are spoken about and how they are treated (e.g. Watters, 2010). We need to be sensitive to cultural differences. Second, we need to assist multilingual students in finding appropriate professionals to help them. This might mean referring students to counseling and psychological services, to advisors who handle students at risk or, in extreme cases, to the campus public safety office. We can show concern and support for students, but if there seems to be a mental health problem, we need to direct the students to professional help.

In addition to variations in manifestations of and reaction to mental health issues, there are other significant differences between multilingual and native English speakers. As might be expected, many international students have difficulty understanding American cultural and educational practices; for example, they may be unfamiliar with the practices of group assignments and peer review and may be reluctant to engage in them. They may mistake the relaxed, friendly manner of authority figures, that is, professors, as meaning that there are few, if any, rules about interacting with faculty. Similarly, they may be confused over the manner of addressing the professor or the US conventions concerning appropriate email.

At the same time, according to Crabtree and Weissberg (2000: 2), international students 'are more often than not strong students – highly motivated, intellectually sophisticated, and self-disciplined'. An internal study (Hafernik & Wiant, 2007) confirms a high level of motivation based on international students' use of out-of-class academic support; in comparing the use of the Writing Center at our institution, international students sought assistance there in greater numbers (55%) than either native speakers (34%) or Gen 1.5 students (41%). In spite of the high degree of motivation to learn English and do well in their studies, we should not expect that they will ever develop the English fluency of a native speaker. In fact, Johns (1999: 170) notes that multilinguals may never display flawless English, but argues that that is acceptable. However, we should encourage the use of campus resources – tutoring, writing centers, speaking centers – to assist them in focusing on 'the big picture'.

International students often come from among the wealthiest families in their home countries. 'Many represent the educational elite of their home countries [and may have attended] the best primary and secondary schools available' (Crabtree & Weissberg, 2000: 2). During the 2010/11 school year, 63.4% of international students listed 'personal and family' as the primary source of income (IIE, 2011). These students often have a sense of economic and social privilege that they bring with them to the US, only to discover that their status does not necessarily translate to the university community (Vandrick, 1995, 2009, 2011). They are often surprised that, in this country of so much wealth and consumerism, not everyone, not even all international students, has the same privilege they do. One of our international students noted that she often had trouble connecting with other international students, citing as an example her classmates' assumption that she, like they, could afford to go to expensive restaurants and nightclubs.

Multilinguals who are US residents (generally immigrants or permanent residents) differ from international students in a number of ways. Researchers (e.g. Ferris, 2009; Reid, 2006) indicate they tend to be less well-educated, and may be conversationally fluent in their native language but lack reading and writing skills. In fact, 'second-generation students may see themselves as bilingual although they have little productive command of a non-English language or designate themselves as native speakers of English when English is their second language' (Harklau et al., 1999: 5). Many were enrolled in bilingual or ESL courses in their elementary and secondary schools and eventually moved to mainstream classes. While they may have difficulty with academic expectations, 'When these students reach college, they may feel strongly that they shouldn't be placed differently from other US high school graduates, and are offended when labeled ESL' (Blanton, 1999: 123).

In pointing out these similarities and differences, we do not wish to essentialize or stereotype students. Within any group (e.g. international, native English speakers, Gen 1.5) there may be as much variation as there is across groups. Although many students in each group understand and practice Western academic and cultural conventions, we have encountered students from each group (including native English speakers) who, for example, seem to not understand how to politely address faculty or seem unfamiliar with certain standard academic practices such as citing sources.

Cultures, Education and Learning Styles

There are, in every society, unstated assumptions about people and how they learn, which act as a set of self-fulfilling prophecies that invisibly guide whatever educational processes may occur there. They act as a kind of unintentional hidden curriculum, or what an anthropologist might call a cultural theory of learning.

Singleton (1995: 8)

Most of us are accustomed to hearing about three learning styles – visual (students who learn best by reading), auditory (those who learn best by hearing) and kinesthetic (those who learn best with a 'hands-on' method). We commonly think of these as checkpoints to make sure our teaching is addressing the needs of all our students or perhaps as diagnostic probes to determine why a student is not succeeding. The way in which one learns is often assumed to be 'fixed', that is, a student always learns best in a particular mode. In fact, learning styles are largely a matter of preference. To understand the diversity among multilingual students on campuses today, we need to take into account not only how they learn in the classroom, but also what role learning styles play in English acquisition. Here, Reid's (2006) distinction between 'ear' learners and 'eye' learners is helpful. As with any continuum, the two ends are extremes (i.e. ear vs. eye learners), with individuals seldom falling neatly at either end. Ear learners are those who learn primarily by listening to lectures, television, tapes and other oral cues. Among multilingual students, US residents who have either immigrated or been born in the US and whose home language is not English tend to be ear learners. Multilingual students who are ear learners typically are orally fluent in their home language but may not be literate in it. Ear learners have learned English mainly through being immersed in the language and culture, mainly through their ears; have graduated from US high schools; and are 'Americanized', understanding US culture, popular culture, current issues and controversies. Although their English listening and speaking skills are excellent, their academic literacy skills may be less developed, displaying features of conversational English and limited academic vocabulary. In some cases, they may have had interrupted education, which also contributes to their limited academic skills.

On the other hand, among multilingual learners, eye learners, those who learn by reading texts, graphs, instructions, charts and the like, are typically international students who are well-educated in their first language and have learned English in a foreign language class, focusing on grammar, vocabulary and language rules. They have learned English through their eyes. They know grammar rules and can talk about the English language and its rules. Their reading skills may be impressive, but their listening and speaking skills may be weaker as they often have had little opportunity to use oral English before coming to the US. Additionally, they may have had little practice in writing English academic essays, their education having focused on rote learning and written exercises (Reid, 2006: 77–79).

In addition to Reid's ear and eye learners, some students are kinesthetic learners – those who learn by doing. This group, like the other two groups, describes both mono-and multilingual students who learn best by the hands-on method. For this group, repeated practice through a combination of reading, writing, speaking and listening may be useful in mastering a concept or skill. This reinforces the knowledge that, for multilingual speakers, sustained practice in settings such as conversation groups, class discussions and informal conversations with the instructor or classmates can be a key factor in developing their understanding and use of English.

One comment we often hear from other faculty members is that multilingual students have difficulty following a lecture, taking class notes or following directions that are given orally. Difficulty in this area can be easily understood – imagine, if you will, that you are listening to a lecture in your second or third language. Most of us would have some difficulty in following every word, understanding the nuances and idioms and adjusting to the speech patterns of the speaker. The implications for testing are obvious. If tests or assignments are based primarily on classroom lectures and oral instructions, the multilingual students are at an obvious disadvantage. They may also be at a disadvantage when assignments or exams are based exclusively on readings without elucidation of the main points by the instructor.

Finally, we must, as Singleton (1995) notes, be attuned to our assumptions and their impact on our teaching. In Chapter 2 there are a number of tips for dealing with a variety of multilingual students' learning styles. However, most students learn by a combination of these strategies, so while we need to be aware of the individual differences in learning styles, this certainly does not mean that we need to present three versions of every lecture or assignment. Rather, classroom activities and assignments that address to some extent each learning style will likely be most useful for all students.

Cultural Patterns and Classroom Practice

Increased campus diversity not only introduces different learning styles and educational experiences but also introduces a host of cultural issues that impact our classrooms. Failure to be aware of these may unintentionally create needless turmoil in the classroom. Although to give a comprehensive list of all the differences we might encounter would be difficult, a few examples illustrate some of the issues that may arise.

One important area in which these differences become manifest is the classroom itself. In many Asian cultures, for example, the classroom is teacher-centered. Students expect that the teacher should be the wise sage, the dispenser of truth. The teacher arrives, lectures and leaves. The students believe they are here to be taught, and they do not see discussions or peer review as learning. Asking questions in class is considered unusual, perhaps even rude, and classroom discussions are infrequent or unknown. In comparing student participation in the United States and in his home country of Korea, a graduate student observes that 'Korean students are more likely to concentrate on lecture and ask questions after the class because they do not want to interrupt the class. There are less interactions between professor and students as well'.

Imagine, then, what happens to this student in a learner-centered classroom in which a variety of methods in addition to lecture may be used, learning is often student directed, the professor indicates that a part of the grade will be based on class participation and students are encouraged to ask questions or even challenge the ideas presented. Despite their unfamiliarity with participating in class, most multilingual students try to adapt. For example, the Korean graduate student quoted above, when discussing class participation adds:

> I worry about what others think about me and what if I ask fool question. I hardly speak during the class; however, we are from foreign country and students who are learning. Even though we are afraid of speaking English in front of others, we need to speak up for better learning. I should open my mouth.

Another cultural concept that has significant implications for education is the role of individual choice. Students in the US choose their teachers, their classes, their schedules and often even the school they attend. Most other countries have a much less flexible system, and in many countries these choices are made for the student by parents or by the school. Similarly, in some cultures, students are told what majors, or even careers, to pursue; their schedules are prepared for them. Students with this type of educational experience may be baffled when an advisor asks, 'What courses do you plan to take next semester?' We have encountered similar difficulties when students are asked to choose a topic for a paper or a speech. Many international students would prefer to have us simply assign a topic; US students, on the other hand, tend to prefer to choose their own topics and are sometimes resentful if we prescribe a particular topic.

A related issue is the role of parents in a student's education. In some countries parents take an active role in their child's education, often acting as an advocate when dealing with teachers and administrators. It can be disconcerting when a parent calls to demand information about the student or requests an explanation of an assignment or a grade. In the United States, such matters come under the Family Educational Rights and Privacy Act (FERPA; US Department of Education, n.d.). Often parents do not understand why we cannot give them the information. In addition, students are not used to advocating or negotiating for themselves. Because of their inexperience, their attempts at advocacy may be perceived as 'pushy'.

Students from relatively restrictive cultures also often have little tolerance for ambiguity. They, as well as some monolingual English-speaking students, may want definitive answers and may be frustrated when we suggest to them that there are a number of acceptable answers to a question or multiple ways to approach an assignment. Additionally, ambiguity or uncertainty is inherent in using English for all but the truly bilingual and bicultural L2 language users. Taking the concept from psychology, Bruder (cited in Ely, 1995: 88) defines the construct of intolerance of ambiguity as 'the tendency to perceive ... ambiguous [novel, complex or insoluble] situations as sources of threat'. Multilingual students may feel uncomfortable in experimenting with new learning strategies and/or novel assignments because they seem risky. They may be unsure what is appropriate in unfamiliar situations. They may be reluctant to ask questions, try new strategies, such as guessing meaning from context, or even speak in class. In discussing language learning, Ely (1995: 93) cautions that very high tolerance for ambiguity, as well as low tolerance of ambiguity, can lead to problems in that such individuals tend to have little concern with linguistic accuracy, so they never attempt to 'master' the finer points of English. He describes the ideal L2 user as one who 'is neither inhibited by low tolerance of ambiguity nor oblivious to linguistic subtleties'.

Another cultural difference that seriously impacts education is private ownership of intellectual property. In some cultures, that is a strange concept indeed. Therefore, plagiarism and copyright violations as defined in Western academe may not be considered a problem. As an example, a recent article in the *San Francisco Chronicle* (Wong, 2010) asserts that plagiarism is widespread in China, particularly in the sciences. Wong profiles Lu Keqian, a former Chinese educator who earns a living by writing papers for students, even graduate students and professors, at an average of $45 US each. Lu justifies his work by saying, 'My opinion is that writing papers for someone else is not wrong . . . . There will always be a time when one needs help from others' (Wong, 2010: A12). One of our Russian students reported that in her culture it is acceptable to help your friends and to do otherwise is considered rude and inappropriate, a concept that extends to studying and completing homework.

These, and other similarities and differences, may not manifest themselves until the students are placed in a classroom setting – context, in this case, is everything. Individual students are always more than a list of similarities and differences. They are just that – individuals – and they will defy every label we try to place upon them. Nevertheless, we hope to offer insight into what you can expect from your students, and what you can do to make your classroom a site of both comfort and learning.

Dispelling the Myths about Multilingual Students in the Classroom

In the course of interviews, phone calls asking for help and informal hallway conversations, as well as remarks overheard from faculty members and from students in compiling the materials for this book, we have come to the realization that both faculty and students have some apprehensions about classes in which multilingual students have been mainstreamed. We end this chapter about 'our students' by examining some common myths and by suggesting how faculty and student concerns can be eased.

Myth 1: Multilingual students will slow the class down

This does not need to be the case. It is true that multilingual students in comparison with native English speakers may take longer to do the reading assignments, may volunteer comments and questions less frequently and may take more time to complete assignments. This does not mean they have to slow down the class; rather it means that multilingual students may have to spend more time outside of class reading and working on assignments and be given more time to make comments in class. For example, they often need time to think and plan before speaking, but this should not be a reason to slow the class down. Instead, try giving the entire class a few minutes to prepare a question or comment, or suggest they make note of the questions they have before class and then bring the questions to class with them.

Myth 2: Multilingual students create resentment on the part of other students

There is no point in denying that some native English speakers are resentful because there are a large number of multilingual students in their classes. This resentment is often bred by misconceptions about other cultures, personal experiences or cultural bias. However, as faculty, we can all help resolve such issues by modeling inclusive practices, encouraging open dialogue and individually (and privately) conferencing with students who may have made inappropriate remarks during class. Ideally there is a balance of non-native and native English speakers in a class. On the whole, we find that most native English speakers are curious about other cultures and both welcome and learn from the different perspectives that multilingual speakers bring to the class.

Myth 3: Multilingual students make group work difficult

Prior planning and preparation for group work minimizes problems in these activities. Spend a bit of time describing the task and assign individual roles for each member of the group. Check in with them occasionally to see if there are any problems developing and that each student is carrying his fair share of the load. Try to see that the contributions of multilingual students are being valued, not overlooked, by the other group members.

Myth 4: Multilingual students' work requires too much time to read and grade

Using checklists, reviewing multiple drafts or referring students to the writing or learning center for assistance can help make the grading easier. However, it should be clear that we advocate grading multilingual students on the same basis as native English speakers. You need not construct special grading criteria for them, nor do you need to correct all the linguistic errors you find. Note only those that interfere with understanding.

Myth 5: Multilingual students don't participate in class; if they do, their comments are unproductive and incomprehensible

Students often need a bit of time to think about and prepare responses. They often have unique insights and perspectives that contribute to class discussions. However, faculty and students must not expect them to have native-like accents. Listeners need to learn to tolerate and understand diverse accents. This is particularly true because the reality of the US today – and the world – is that more and more of us must interact with individuals who speak English with an accent different from our own. The key question is whether students can communicate their ideas.

Myth 6: Multilingual students don't know about the US and the topics covered in class

A difficulty that professors have with all university students is determining what knowledge students do and do not have; in other words, what content is common knowledge and what assumptions can we make about students' knowledge? It may be true that multilingual students lack some knowledge about events in American history or about the US Constitution or system of government, but international students as well as multilingual students who have attended some high school in the United States frequently know a great deal about American popular culture, culled mostly from television, movies and the internet, and, for permanent residents, from their friends. Multilingual students tend to be eager to learn more. It is also true that multilingual students generally know a great deal about their own cultures and/or countries, have had many experiences and offer unique perspectives. It is good to allow them to write or speak about their own cultures and perspectives when appropriate; they have much to teach all of us.

Myth 7: Multilingual students simply need to try harder and spend more time studying

This is true for some multilingual students the same as it is true for certain native English-speaking students. However, the majority of multilingual students that we have encountered work hard, spending many hours studying and preparing for their classes. Most are willing to put in the time to do well in their courses. Multilingual students are no less capable, and sometimes a great deal more capable, than native speakers in our classes.

Myth 8: Faculty need special training to teach multilingual students

Not true. Faculty may need special training to teach English or composition skills to multilinguals, but that is not the case for faculty who teach history, science, math, philosophy, sociology, literature or any of the other myriad subjects offered in our colleges and universities. Faculty in the disciplines teach content in their professional fields, generally not English.

This book is designed to assist faculty across the disciplines to integrate multilingual students into their classrooms, to help all students be successful and to help all students learn from each other. These are our students – as Shaughnessy (1998: 7) says, 'They are here'. We encourage our faculty colleagues to see them, not as a problem but as a resource and opportunity.

2 Constructing Classrooms Where Students Can Succeed

A faculty member walks into her first class of the semester with a sense of anticipation. She quickly scans the room, noticing a multitude of faces, only a few of which are familiar. She sees that in the class different ethnicities and ages are represented and that the class seems to have slightly more females than males. Questions quickly run through her head: (1) 'How will the first day go?' (2) 'Do students want to be in this class?' and (3) 'Will this class and the semester go well?' Putting these and more questions aside, she introduces herself and gives an overview of the class. The semester begins.

Anyone who has taught understands the above scenario. No matter how long one has been teaching, the first day of a new semester is accompanied by questions about how the class will go and a quick take of the new class. As the semester unfolds, more questions arise and faculty are constantly making decisions and making adjustments based on students' needs and other variables. Certainly, all teaching situations are not the same. Courses differ widely along a number of variables: size, content, goals and objectives, assessment tools used, level of the course, faculty characteristics, student characteristics and more. Yet, a few things remain the same, notably that by and large faculty are passionate about their disciplines and about teaching. Additionally, most faculty want each student to be successful, not only in their courses but also in the university and their future endeavors. Faculty take pride in their students' accomplishments and feel disappointed when students do not succeed. In short, faculty care about their disciplines, about student learning and about students as individuals.

As more multilingual and ethnically diverse students arrive on our campuses, faculty face new challenges. Faculty may welcome them into their classrooms, but they may feel unsure how best to make them an integral part of the class and how to assist those who seem to have difficulty. Some faculty may instinctively know how to help multilingual students be successful; others learn strategies through trial and error; still others may never feel they have a handle on helping multilingual students; and others may wish multilingual students would go away and come back after they have 'fixed any linguistic problems' and 'learned how to be good students'. In this chapter, we outline strategies to help faculty working with multilingual students: to make explicit what they may do instinctively. At the same time, we offer faculty opportunities to reflect on their teaching practices, refine their knowledge of challenges multilingual students face and gain insight into what strategies may be effective. Underlying our discussion are several basic questions: how can we create an environment where all students can succeed, where students feel challenged yet comfortable at the same time? How do multilingual students feel on campus and in our classrooms? Is the campus climate welcoming? How can we integrate multilingual students into the academy, help them learn and increase their chances of success? We begin by outlining fundamentals of second language (L2) acquisition, especially of L2 academic language, and then offer general advice for creating classrooms that foster student success.

Fundamentals of L2 Acquisition with a Focus on Academic Language

(1) Languages are dynamic and connected to their contexts and to their users

Linguistic texts such Curzan and Adams (2012) note three distinctive features of language: (a) It is systematic, that is, it is rule-governed; (b) Language is arbitrary. There is often no logic to the rules. For example, there is generally no direct relationship between a word and its meaning. Why is a pencil called a *pencil*? Why isn't it called a *teapot*? The answer is simple: a community of speakers has agreed that *pencil* is the word that we use and not the word *teapot*. A word's meaning is based on conventional understandings by a group of speakers; (c) Language is creative and evolves. Using a language means understanding new utterances and sentences and creating novel utterances. Also, evidence of language's creativity is around us every day. For example, in English we often make new verbs by changing nouns into verbs. An example is the word *friend*. Until the advent and subsequent popularity of social networking, *friend* was only used as a noun. Now, however, *friend* is commonly used as a verb to mean to add someone as a friend on a social network site. A common question is 'Will you *friend* me?'.

These distinctive features, along with others, are found in each language and, of course, each language is a different system with different rules and constituent parts. Here we do not wish to provide a crash course in linguistics but rather to emphasize the complexity and the evolutionary nature of language. Language is not a closed, static system but is dynamic and constantly changing and adapting to the context and situations in which it is used. Language is embedded in social context and social practices (Benesch, 2009; Curzan & Adams, 2012; Heath, 1983). Therefore, language cannot be acquired simply by studying and learning constituent features (e.g. vocabulary, grammar) objectively. True, to 'know' English one must have command of the sound system (phonology), word formation (morphology), lexicon or vocabulary (semantics), grammar (syntax) and discourse (larger units of communication than the sentence level). Using a language effectively is much more. It entails hard-to-quantify elements such as knowing when to use or not use certain expressions, interpreting units of speech/reading beyond simply adding up the meaning of each word, and understanding an author's intended meaning. In short, much more than 'book learning' is needed to master a language, and this is especially true of language used in academic contexts.

(2) Identity plays an important role in language acquisition

Lave and Wenger (1991: 53) argue that 'learning involves the construction of identities'. Others researching the relationship between identity and language learning contend that this relationship is complex and little understood (e.g. Chiang & Schmida, 1999; Harklau, 2000; Norton, 1997). Norton (2000: 132) argues that 'Learning an L2 is not simply a skill that is acquired with hard work and dedication, but a complex social practice that engages the identities of language learners in ways that have received little attention in the field of Second Language Acquisition.' Wenger (1998: 154) emphasizes that identity is not static, but is continually constructed and forms what he calls 'trajectories', not a path but a 'continuous motion . . . . It [trajectory] has a coherence through time that connects the past, the present, and the future' (Wenger, 1998: 154).

Typically, adolescence and young adulthood are considered important periods in individual identity formation. When individuals come to college, they are often away from home and on their own for the first time and in an unfamiliar environment: they face new personal, social and academic challenges and responsibilities. In addition to juggling the roles monolingual English speakers are required to do (e.g. child, adult, student, friend, employee), multilingual students must negotiate a multi-cultural identity. How do they negotiate between their first language (L1) and English? How do they see their identities as language users? Do they feel like different people when they use their L1 or English? What are their language practices? Do they code-switch (move easily from one language to another) or translanguage (a term that includes code-switching but goes beyond it, focusing on language practices that multilinguals use 'to make sense of their bilingual worlds' [García, 2009: 45])? If so, when and with whom (e.g. do they use their L1 with family and English with friends and at school)? Do they translanguage in various domains and within single domains? Which groups do students feel they belong to? Which groups do they wish to belong to? How a student answers these questions, largely subconsciously and indirectly, affects her motivation, effort and success in academe as well as in general US society.

Jun Yang (2010), having come to the United States from China only four years before entering college, describes her life. 'I am lost, lost in between my two conflictive natures. . . . Having spent my childhood in China and a large percentage of my teenage years here make neither side of me comprehendible. One plus one never equals two lives to me, but a zero' (Yang, 2010: 51). Yang goes on to describe her difficulties with English: pronunciation is at times problematic but more problematic are idiomatic expressions (e.g. 'under the weather') and cultural references (e.g. Oprah Winfrey, rules of baseball), not the basic linguistic skills of listening, speaking, reading and writing. At the same time, Yang worries about losing her Chinese literacy and knowledge of current topics and events in China. Using her parents' Chinese dialect at home and English in public and with friends, she feels that she does not belong to any group and says:

> I am walking back and forth between these two roles I play and trying to look for the one that I truly belong to. What is my identity? I am stuck on the intersection of the two paths and do not know what to do and where to go. I need a direction to follow. These conflicts between my two cultures and natures make me undefined. So I am seeking and trying my best to figure a way out and put these pieces of the puzzles together. (Yang, 2010: 53)

Others (e.g. Shen, 1998; Zawacki & Habib, 2010) also write about the need to reinvent themselves to have an academic identity in English and how gaining such an identity means leaving some aspects of themselves (e.g. their academic identities in their other languages) behind. Shen (1998) writes about how he had to 'redefine himself' which meant not only being his Chinese self but also creating an 'English identity'.

Multilingual students permanently resident in the US, such as Yang, may struggle more with defining themselves than international students, who typically have established their identity and are sojourners in the United States, so their 'home' and 'native country' identities may more easily be balanced as they can keep them more distinct, less entangled.

Identity formation is complex and plays a role in how comfortable an individual feels in academic situations, social communities and in US society in general. Wenger (1998: 146) contends 'Building an identity consists of negotiating the meanings of our experience of membership in social communities' (Wenger, 1998: 146). Emphasizing that it is a 'mistaken dichotomy to wonder whether the unit of analysis of identity should be the community or the person', he argues that 'it is as misleading to view identities as abstractly collective as it is to view them as narrowly individual' (Wenger, 1998: 147). Later we return to the subject of student identities when discussing students' integration into the academy.

(3) Everyday language and academic language are very different

A distinction is made between two types of language use: (1) Basic Interpersonal Communication Skills (BICS) and (2) Cognitive Academic Language Proficiency (CALP) (Cummins, 1979; Cummins & Swain, 1986). BICS are acquired naturally by children who develop normally in their first language (L1) and can generally be acquired in a second language (L2) in a relatively short period of time when individuals are in a natural setting where the language is used. Linguists agree that by the age of six, normally developing children in rich linguistic environments have acquired the basics of that language, whatever language it is, and are competent users of that language (Curzan & Adams, 2012; Pinker, 1994). CALP consists of academic language skills such as advanced vocabulary, grammar knowledge, articulation of ideas and strong literacy skills. Unlike BICS, CALP requires much longer to develop in L1 and L2, and in some individuals it never develops adequately (Collier, 1987, 1989; Scarcella, 1996, 2003). Estimates are that it takes a minimum of seven years, under good conditions, for individuals to acquire CALP (Collier, 1987, 1989). A term that overlaps with CALP is 'academic literacy' which Ogbu (1990: 520) defines as 'the ability to read and write and compute in the form taught and expected in formal education. Put differently, I consider literacy to be synonymous with academic performance'. Even if CALP is not well developed and academic performance seems weak, students are still capable of critical thinking and abstract reasoning.

Whereas many multilingual students, especially those who are born or largely raised or schooled in the US, may be fluent in English but less proficient in academic skills, typically international students, those holding student visas are privileged and well-educated and have acquired academic literacy in one or more languages before coming to an English academic environment (Vandrick, 1995). Therefore, international students' general academic knowledge may transfer to the English academic situation. The rules and conventions vary from language to language but individuals literate in one language understand the concept of academic literacy, whereas individuals who lack academic literacy in any language, whether a first or second language, may not have this understanding (Ferris, 2009; Reid, 2006).

The advantages that students who are educated and literate in their L1 have over those who have less developed L1 literacy skills can be explained in part by Cummins' (2000) idea of a Common Underlying Proficiency (CUP). According to the CUP model, languages that an individual knows rely on a common, not a separate, underlying language proficiency. Conceptual knowledge transfers and does not have to be relearned. To visually explain the CUP model, 'Cummins gives us the image of a *dual iceberg*, with the surface features of the two languages separated at the top level where they are visible, but like an iceberg, emerging from the same source' (García, 2009: 69).

Whether an individual is an international student or a US multilingual student, academic literacy is complex and hard to define. Ferris (2009: 26) synthesizes the research of Kern (2000), Scarcella (2003) and Singhal (2004) to assert that academic language proficiency has three interacting dimensions: linguistic, cognitive and sociocultural/psychological. Each of these dimensions is multifaceted, and even native English speakers may not gain proficiency in academic literacy. Acquiring academic literacy is a slow and arduous journey.

(4) Multilingual students do not become 'native' English speakers. A few courses will not perfect students' English

Roberge (2009: 6) says the notion of language remediation is based on a *myth of transience*, a belief that students travel from being learners of English to being completely competent in English. This term *the myth of transience* was coined by Rose (1985) to refer to the belief that students who have a perceived deficiency in writing skills (e.g. low literacy skills) only need one or two courses to remediate or 'fix' this lack, and then students will be competent writers in all areas of academe. Stanley (2010) points out that this myth of transience is evident in the idea and rhetoric of remediation that are applied not only to writing ability but also to math ability and general language ability. An assumption about multilingual students whose first language is not English, as well as about those who have not mastered the preferred form of English, is that a few classes targeted at their weaknesses or 'problem areas' will make them 'whole'. It is unrealistic to believe that multilingual students will become native English speakers. Throughout their academic careers, multilingual students, like native English speakers, continue to improve their academic language proficiency and academic skills. We, as faculty, can help them in this process but can't assume that students will become native English speakers. In fact, questions about who owns English and the definitions of native speaker and non-native speaker are controversial (e.g. Canagarajah, 1999; Kramsch, 1997; Widdowson, 1994). Such questions are even more relevant as English spreads around the world as a global language and more varieties of English (i.e. Englishes) are used (e.g. Indian English, Singaporean English, European Union English). Multilingual students may have a good command of English and, in fact, be native speakers of an English, just not 'our English'. Canagarajah (2006: 217) cautions us not to assume that globalization leads to a homogeneous world where difference doesn't matter. He argues 'Issues of power and difference have simply become more subtle and dispersed.'

Another area where the term *myth of transience* has been used is in examining writing in the disciplines or specific academic fields. Russell (2002) argues that academic writing has historically been seen as a 'generalizable, elementary skill and that academia held a universal, immutable standard of literacy . . . and that writing was simply a form of talking rather than a complex and developing response to a community's discourse – a mode of learning, in other words' (Russell, 2002: 6). From this view, a simple solution (i.e. a course or two on writing) can 'fix' students' poor writing, and then students are able to be proficient writers in any field of study. That is, if one can write well in one course, one can write well in all courses and all disciplines. This belief is simply a myth.

General Advice

(1) Cultivate within yourself an orientation to look at students' potential and their abilities, not only at their differences and challenges

Rose (2005) argues, as do others, that students are often judged not by what they do well, but by what they do *not* do well. Faculty may comment on students' poor grammar or lack of what they perceive as good study habits and skills, not recognizing their original ideas or creative use of language. Roberge (2009: 5) writes, 'Students are seen as "learners of English" rather than "users of English".' Roberge, along with other researchers (e.g. Freire, 1970; Kutz *et al.*, 1993; Rose, 1985), encourages us to build on what students bring to classes and to encourage students to discover and develop their abilities and competencies. Adopting this attitude means rejecting the difference-as-deficit and difference-as-estrangement perspectives, perspectives that see difference as a problem (difference-as-deficit), something to be fixed or difference as an alienating factor (difference-as-estrangement), preventing individuals from being academically successful. Individuals are seen as trapped in their linguistic and cultural worlds (Canagarajah, 2006: 218). Canagarajah (2006) argues that the difference-as-resource perspective provides more complexity than either of the other attitudes. This perspective values what each student brings: her experience, cultural knowledge, values and beliefs. In discussing critical writing, Canagarajah asserts that:

> Multilingual students do – and can – use their background as a stepping-stone to master academic discourses. Their values can function as a source of strength in their writing experience in English, enabling them to transfer many skills from their traditions of vernacular communication .... We should respect and value the linguistic and cultural peculiarities our students may display, rather than suppressing them. (Canagarajah, 2006: 218)

Although Canagarajah is speaking of writing skills, his comments are equally relevant to other language and academic skills.

(2) Avoid making assumptions about students, about their knowledge, abilities and experiences

Closely related to treating each student as an individual is avoiding making assumptions about students and labeling or categorizing them. Assumptions can go either way, positive or negative, but by their nature fail to give a full picture of the individual, her knowledge and her experiences. In her article, '"You are beginning to sound like an academic": Finding and owning your academic voice', Tracey Costley (2008), a British student studying in a graduate program in the US, discusses how being given the label 'first generation student' bewildered her, impacted her perception of herself and created barriers she had to overcome to find her voice. In arguing that labels such as 'first generation student' create binary oppositions, she writes, 'Ultimately, the dynamic that results is that there are students who at enrolment are considered, on the basis of their socio-economic and ethnic backgrounds, to be in deficit and those who are considered to be "in credit"' (Costley, 2008: 77). Assumptions about Asian students, especially Asian

American students, being the 'model minority' (i.e. hard working, smart students, especially good at math) also place pressure on students and create barriers for individuals. Spack (1997: 765) cautions us against labeling multilingual students regardless of our intentions: 'But even if our reasons are well intentioned, we need to consider that, in the process of labeling students, we put ourselves in the powerful position of rhetorically constructing their identities, a potentially hazardous enterprise.'

Assumptions about multilingual students tend to be tied to their language abilities and perceived socio-economic status, which may also be based on their language use. A student who seems to struggle speaking English is often assumed to be less intelligent than one who is articulate. Four closely related assumptions seem common: (a) assumptions about a student's ability or intellect; (b) assumptions about a student's interest, effort and motivation; (c) assumptions about a student's background knowledge of and experiences with the subject matter; and (d) assumptions about a student's knowledge of and experience with academic literacy and Western academic practices. The first two assumptions can be counteracted by keeping an open mind, by getting data and information about each student throughout the semester, by assessing her work and through private conversations. For example, a quiet international student who seldom speaks in class and appears to be lost may earn the highest score on the first written assignment or midterm, whereas an articulate multilingual student who actively participates in class may do less well on written assignments. It's hard to read students and gauge their comprehension, engagement and ability. A brief scenario illustrates this point. The first week of the semester, a faculty member spoke to her chair about a male student who seemed bored in her writing class for multilingual students. She felt he might benefit from a higher level writing course and be more challenged. The chair suggested that the instructor watch the student closely until the end of the week, gather samples of the student's work and then come back to speak to her again. The next day, the student, about whom the instructor had expressed concern, came to see the chair. He said that his courses were going well, but in one course the content was particularly difficult and he wondered if he would be able to keep up. When asked which course he found difficult, he explained that it was his writing course. The faculty member had misread the student. It is easy for faculty to misread students as not being interested in their studies or in being unable to handle the material when, in fact, they may be dealing with personal issues or other obligations, such as work or family, which disrupt their studies. Students are often confronting many issues outside their academic studies that make them appear unmotivated or uninterested. At the same time as avoiding making assumptions about our students and their abilities, we want to identify those who may need additional support as soon as possible. Thus, getting information from students directly and indirectly can help identify such students.

More common than making assumptions about an individual's ability or motivation, we make assumptions about what students do or don't know, their background knowledge and their familiarity with academic literacy and US academic practices. This can be problematic for all students, yet is especially so for multicultural students who may not have a grounding in Western culture and academic practices. Here we are not talking about knowledge gained in prerequisite courses that will apply to upper division courses in a discipline (e.g. calculus, anatomy, accounting, inorganic chemistry). In order to fully understand textbooks, readings, lectures and assignments, students often need background knowledge about the topic or issue, information that may be cultural and Western. Lacking schema or background knowledge about the general subject area may put students at a disadvantage, especially if students see little connection to their knowledge and experiences. For example, an international student told us of his inability to answer an essay question on a marketing exam because he didn't know what the Super Bowl was. Yang (2010) provides another simple example of the need for background knowledge from her high school gym class. When playing baseball, she hit a home run, but not knowing much about the game, did not touch the bases as she ran them, despite her classmates repeatedly yelling at her to 'touch the bases'. Her home run didn't count and her team lost the game.

Assuming that multilingual students cannot handle certain tasks because they don't have the requisite knowledge can also be problematic, though less common. For example, a faculty member of a communication course argued that his international students could not handle a group project in which they had to research a problem in the local community and then propose a solution. He argued that the international students didn't know anything about the community or common practices in the United States. This argument seems to underestimate students' abilities and experiences. Furthermore, it assumes that those unfamiliar with US communities will have no insights to offer when, in fact, they may offer a new perspective and new avenue into local problems.

Assumptions about what multilingual students *do* know about US academic practices can also be harmful. This is often true also for students perceived as 'mainstream'. In courses where students have mastered the subject content previously or have sufficient background knowledge, they may still not be conversant with Western academic practices, or there may be cultural value clashes. Things that faculty take for granted may not be obvious to multilingual or even English monolingual students. Multilingual students may have different values, beliefs, behaviors, motivations and practices that conflict with US academic beliefs, values and practices (e.g. Ferris, 2009; Kern, 2000; Scarcella, 2003). For example, students may not know how to politely address faculty in person or in emails. They may not be aware of what the standard academic formatting for written assignments is or how to respectfully ask questions or make requests of faculty. Classroom practices may also differ as Flaitz (2003, 2006) illustrates in her books about educational practices, beliefs and values in other countries. For example, Flaitz (2003: 104) points out that in the People's Republic of China (PRC), students do not like to be singled out for praise, yet do enjoy performing. In addition to these seemingly minor issues, there is a tradition of valuing original work, and individuality, in the US that differs in other countries. In writing about creating an English identity, Shen (1998: 124) asserts that the first rule in English composition is 'Be yourself'. Shen goes on to say that 'In China, the "I" is always subordinated to the "We" – be it the working class, the Party, the country or some other collective body' (Shen, 1998: 124). Similarly, Flaitz (2003) notes that students in the PRC are not expected to voice their opinions or reactions to issues presented in class. Flaitz attributes this to 'the widely shared belief that young people are far too inexperienced to generate responses that would sound interesting, or worthy of attention' (Flaitz, 2003: 104). Indeed, we have had Chinese students ask us how they can possibly have an opinion about an important topic on which many scholars have so eloquently written. The clash between the importance the West places on individuality and the value other cultures place on collectivism and authority seems related to the issue of citing and documenting sources and even the important issue of academic integrity, the definition of which is culturally based (Pennycook, 1996; Pennycook et al., 2004).

(3) If possible, get to know your students

Faculty can get to know their students on a variety of levels and in different ways. The ease with which this can be done is often determined by the size of the class and the workload of the faculty member. In a large economics class of 150, it seems unlikely that a faculty member will know all the students' names or information about each one. Conversely, in a writing course with 20 students, faculty can quickly learn each student's name and get to know each one to some extent. Even in classes with as many as 50 students, faculty may learn students' names and the correct pronunciation of them. Faculty often quickly learn the faces and perhaps names of students who ask questions or make comments in class, come to office hours, contribute to course blogs or discussion boards, or email with questions. Most faculty can recognize students who are in their classes and greet them when they see them on campus. Even in large classes, students can be treated as individuals by small acts from professors that show the professor is interested in the individual.

The type of class, its goals and its size determine how much interaction there is among students and faculty. There are, however, practices that faculty can build into their classes to connect with and get to know their students. Examples of systematic things that faculty can do include (a) conducting a quick online survey before class begins or early in the semester, asking about their major, class level (e.g. freshmen, sophomore), reasons for taking the course, languages they know, home language and other information specific to the course (e.g. previous courses in the discipline); (b) having students briefly introduce themselves to each other in class or online; (c) having each student create a webpage on a course management system; (d) meeting with each student to discuss a major assignment or project either individually or in small groups; (e) encouraging students to come to office hours; and (f) taking opportunities that arise to find out about a student or students (e.g. during an office visit asking a student about how the semester is going or having a general conversation about college life). A faculty member in the natural sciences noted that he feels it is important to meet with students, especially international students, and let them know he is approachable. He commented that he often does this before the class begins.

In sum, students are individuals and as Norton Peirce (1995: 25–26) points out, 'the individual language learner is not ahistorical and unidimensional but has a complex and sometimes contradictory social identity, changing across time and space'.

(4) Help students become members of the academy

Adjusting to life as a university student is difficult for all students, but this is especially true for multilingual students, whether they are international students or US residents. Multilingual students may feel like strangers in the social and cultural environments on campus. They may not have an understanding of what is expected of them inside and outside the classroom. They may not have any understanding of how the community operates, who the major players are, or basically know the 'rules of the game'. They may have more pressure and family expectations placed on them, may have to work more to pay tuition and living expenses, and may have weaker study and time management skills. Harklau (2000), when talking about the transition from high school to college for Gen 1.5 students, notes that basically the rules learned in high school may not apply in college. Because of these changing rules, students are often confused and may flounder. In high school, hard work and diligence are components of grades and these traits are rewarded, whereas in college more focus is placed on the quality of the finished product (e.g. the essay, the exam grade, the speech) with little attention to the effort exerted. In fact, faculty may say, as we have, that the time spent doing an assignment does not factor into the grade, rather the results are what matter. Additionally, Harklau notes that these Gen 1.5 students who have successfully completed high school in the United States, frequently having moved out of high school ESL courses and into all 'regular' courses, often may be lumped with new international students in classes and may even be placed into ESL university courses. The institution and faculty sometimes fail to acknowledge the vast experience with and understanding of US culture and society that these students have. Faculty and others may even ask these Gen 1.5 students 'How is this done in your country?' not realizing that their country is the United States.

Whose responsibility is it to help students understand the workings of the academy, adjust to it, and become full participating members? The answer is 'Everyone's'. Each of us can ease the transition for students by simply making what we take for granted explicit for students. Simple acts include announcing lectures and events on campus that are related to the course; taking students on a library tour or giving an assignment that must be completed in the library; announcing support services and events available on campus such as the writing and speaking center, peer tutoring programs, study skills workshops, student clubs, career services workshops and fairs, counseling and psychological services and free community events.

In our classes, we should not assume that students know, for example, whether Wikipedia is or is not an acceptable resource for a paper for our class. If we do not allow Wikipedia, we need to tell students that. If a student uses an inappropriate email salutation or closing (e.g. misspells the instructor's name, addresses the professor by last name only, begins with 'Yo', ends with 'I love you'), we can point out how such a greeting or closing affects us and the impression it leaves as well as offer appropriate alternatives. In sum, by helping students understand what is expected, what behaviors the community values, what the community has to offer, how the academy is structured and how it operates, we can help them become a part of it.

As we seek to make our classes more inclusive and accepting of multilingual students, we remain cognizant of the fact that we as individual faculty members do not operate in a vacuum. Rather we operate within the broader context of our universities that in turn operate within the broader social and cultural context.

(5) Help students become insiders in their disciplines

To be academically successful, not only do students need to become members of the university and feel they belong, they need to become active participants ('insiders') in their specific disciplines. A belief that possessing general academic skills, such as writing and speaking well, can bring success in all courses and disciplines is inadequate. Indeed, Russell (2002: 21–22) contends that only in a broad context do members of the academy today 'share a single set of linguistic conventions and traditions of inquiry'. Rather he asserts that each discipline has its own specific discourse, traditions and norms. Certainly, we can easily recognize that writing a literary analysis of *The Great Gatsby* does not require the same linguistic and rhetorical skills as writing up a research project in computer science. It also seems obvious that the same basic linguistic skills are needed in both (i.e. a knowledge of the structure of English sentences and conventions of punctuation). Nonetheless, one needs much more than these common basic skills and knowledge to become members of a specific discipline. How do students become a part of a discipline-specific discourse community? How do they learn how to do things like insiders in the discipline do? How do they move from neophyte to competent member in a field of study?

Several terms and theories, applied to discipline-specific environments and at times to the academy broadly, have been used to describe the process of individuals moving from being novices to experts. Examples include (a) initiation into the community (e.g. Bizzell, 1982); (b) 'inventing the university' (Bartholomae, 2003); and (c) sociocultural genre studies, studies about the constituents and features of discipline-specific academic discourse (Berkenkotter & Huckin, 1995; Swales, 1990). Although each has a different focus, all of these have similarities: they view academic discipline-specific discourse, writing and speaking as socially situated and they view individuals becoming members of a discipline as a socialization process.

One concept that we find particularly helpful is the apprenticeship model or what Lave and Wenger (1991) call a 'community of practice'.

Embracing the concept of communities of practice means that we consider learning in social terms. Lave and Wenger argue that the academic community is similar to other communities such as insurance claim processors or midwives. With this sociocultural perspective, Wenger (1998) argues that social participation is learning and that:

> Participation here refers not just to local events of engagement in certain activities with certain people, but to a more encompassing process of being active participants in the *practices* of social communities and constructing *identities* in relation to these communities . . . . Such participation shapes not only what we do, but also how we are and how we interpret what we do. (Wenger, 1998: 4)

This sociocultural orientation sees learning as situated in specific, local contexts and emphasizes the need for novices to have access to experts in the discipline in structured and unstructured situations. Barton and Tusting (2005: 2) assert that important to the 'fundamental process of learning' is co-participation by new members and experts, even if novices participate only peripherally. While some have criticized the apprenticeship model and communities of practice framework as simplistic and unrealistic in their view of environments as being open and welcoming, we believe they do capture how neophytes become members and experts in an academic discipline. The concept of 'communities of practice' emphasizes that a novice learns how to be a biologist, for example, by 'doing science' even if not very well, by having experts guide her while working alongside her, and by participating in a community of biologists.

Bartholomae (2003) argues that students must 'invent the university' for themselves and they do this by:

> [M]imicking its language, finding some compromise between idiosyncrasy, a personal history, and the requirements of convention, the history of a discipline. They must learn to speak our language. Or they must dare to speak it, or to carry off the bluff, since speaking and writing will most certainly be required long before the skill is 'learned'. (Bartholomae, 2003: 403)

He goes on to explain that students must 'imagine for themselves the privilege of being "insiders"' and imagine that they have the right to speak and be heard. 'The students, in effect, have to assume privilege without having any'. (Bartholomae, 2003: 408)

While becoming insiders in the academy and a specific discipline, multilingual students can influence, and often change, the academic environment and disciplines. In short, they can become agents of change. 'They transform the communities by critically and consciously resisting and changing the existing ways of doing things, and more often, by simply being who they are, by bringing their ways of living and coping into the mix' (Li & Casanave, 2008: 6).

We, as faculty, need to encourage multilingual students to assume privilege and welcome them to our communities of practice while at the same time being open to our communities changing and evolving because of them.

(6) Cultivate intellectual curiosity in students

As faculty, we seek to spark students' interest and encourage them to embrace new ideas, take more responsibility for their own learning, venture into areas not specifically covered in our classes and find their passion. Countless stories are told by individuals about how one person, often a faculty member, opened new vistas for them, vistas that led them to eventually pursue a certain subject area or career path. Simple things make a difference. One of the most obvious ways faculty stimulate students' intellectual curiosity is through their enthusiasm, knowledge and love for their subject. A faculty member's enthusiasm and interest in learning and discovering new knowledge are infectious. Students know when a faculty member is excited about the subject and loves the discipline. Individual faculty have found different ways of successfully engaging students and motivating them, taking into account their own personal styles and the discipline. In short, how do we help students find their interests and develop intrinsic motivation, a desire to learn for the pleasure and joy of it, rather than rely on external motivation, a desire to earn a good grade, please the professor, or do what others want?

The following list of possible ways to spark students' interest is by no means exhaustive. Indeed, each reader should add to the list, but a few general ways we have found useful include:

(1) Exposing students to a multitude of experiences and materials (e.g. through technology, guest speakers, different media, group work, case studies and conferences).
(2) Making connections, and encouraging students to do the same, between the subject matter and students' lives, experiences and knowledge

(e.g. by bringing in current events related to the course, by discussing connections explicitly, by asking students to make connections explicitly).

(3) Inventing opportunities for intellectual curiosity (e.g. problem sets, problem solving, probing questions).

(4) Providing assignments that give students some latitude to explore personal interests within the subject area (e.g. by allowing students to choose a narrow research topic within a broad area; by having students choose a topic and requiring them to use a specific resource; by giving students a set of problems/questions and asking them to choose a given percentage, say 75%, of them).

In this chapter, we have provided a framework for thinking about how to integrate multilingual students into our classrooms as well as offered general advice for making our classrooms inclusive environments in which all students can succeed. In the next part, we move on to specific ways that faculty can build on this information, and we discuss strategies to use in our courses.

Part 2

Understanding and Addressing Language Skills

Introduction

One of the biggest problems for non-native speakers of English is listening comprehension. It's hard to tell if multilingual students understand the lectures and the class discussions.
Business professor

The reading load is heavy in US universities. It seems that you have a lot of free time, but it isn't true because there is a lot of reading to do for classes.
Undergraduate student from Italy

Multilingual students tend to have trouble articulating and supporting their opinions.
Science professor

One of the challenges I face in classes is writing essays in English. I never wrote essays in English before.
Undergraduate student from Mexico

The quotations above from faculty and students comment on the importance of the four basic language skills: listening, reading, speaking and writing. Whatever the disciplines, competency in these language skills is required for academic success. Different fields of study, however, may place more emphasis on one or two language skills over the others. Surveys of and interviews with faculty about what skills students need to be successful in the academy, in general, and in specific disciplines and professions, in particular, confirm that particular strengths are often valued more in certain fields (Ferris & Tagg, 1996; Johns, 1981; Olster, 1980). For example, in interviews with faculty we heard from an art professor that 'The currency in the art world is writing, so accuracy is very important.' In health sciences, importance is placed on being able to analyze and critique a situation from oral and written information and then being able to firmly and respectfully give one's critique orally to colleagues and supervisors. Often this needs to be done on the spot, with little time for reflection and consultation with others. In business, emphasis is often placed on teamwork, which entails careful listening, responding, negotiating and cooperating with others to complete a task.

Just as certain disciplines and even individual faculty place more importance on certain academic language skills, students face different language and academic challenges and may value specific skills over others. For example, one of our Asian graduate students in education feels it is important to sound like a native speaker and speak idiomatic English. She contends that speaking well allows one to interact with native English speakers, something she feels is most important for her. Other Asian graduate students find questioning and challenging the ideas of others, both students' and faculty's ideas, most difficult. They comment that in their countries expressing one's ideas in writing and in speaking is not seen as important; rather, it is important to express the ideas of authorities. A European undergraduate notes that written exams and writing academic essays present a new challenge because the norm in many European universities is oral exams, exams lasting several hours in fact. In addition to individual students' perceptions of what skills are most important is the reality that students have individual strengths and weaknesses. A student may be verbally articulate, displaying excellent comprehension, while at the same time her written work may lack grammatical accuracy and sophisticated vocabulary. Another student may speak haltingly and seem not to understand what is being said but may write fluently and accurately with a distinct voice.

Philosophical questions about language have long intrigued humans as have practical questions such as 'What do humans do when they use language, that is, when they listen, speak, read, or write?' Here we are concerned with the practical questions about what individuals do when they use language in academic environments. Academic demands placed on students today are different, perhaps more complicated, than in the past. No longer are students asked to read only print material that proceeds in a linear fashion from beginning to end, nor are they asked to write using only print sources and their own ideas. Instead, students and faculty are using technologies and reading and writing in cyberspace. We are reading texts online and clicking on hyperlinks, thereby reading in a nonlinear fashion. We are reading and writing blogs, wikis, tweets, websites and much more. We are also listening and speaking in new ways, using technologies such as chatting online, watching videos online, computer simulations, virtual communities, and collaborating via Skype and other technologies. Technologies have impacted the academy, the way we teach, the expectations we have of students and, some would argue, the way we think (Carr, 2008; Turkle, 2004). For example, do we have shorter attention spans for reading and listening? It seems that technologies and media today do not encourage sustained communication and thought. Therefore, we must take technologies and the demands they have created into account when thinking about student learning and our teaching.

In this introductory chapter, we outline the types of knowledge students need to use language successfully, discuss the common groupings of individual language skills, and provide a few general thoughts on understanding and addressing students' language skills.

Types of Knowledge Students Need to be Academically Successful

To be academically successful, individuals need several types of knowledge: linguistic, pragmatic and schematic (background knowledge). First, individuals need to have an internalized system that includes linguistic knowledge (knowledge of syntax, the sound system, the morphology system, semantics and lexicon) and pragmatic knowledge, sometimes called communicative knowledge (knowledge of how to accomplish something with language and do it appropriately, taking into account the context). Perhaps the most obvious linguistic knowledge that students need is of grammar and vocabulary. Faculty, as well as students, often comment on students' lack of grammatical accuracy and their limited vocabulary. The 'threshold hypothesis' (Grabe, 2001) suggests language proficiency, especially as regards syntax and vocabulary, plays a major role in reading abilities and writing abilities. The proficiency threshold does not mean mastery of a specific set of grammatical structures or vocabulary items, but rather the proficiency threshold is variable depending upon task, text and reader (Grabe, 2001: 32). For example, listening to a formal lecture in chemistry may require less general language proficiency than participating in a class discussion in a sociology class. Similarly, a calculus class may require less general language proficiency than a philosophy class. When examining vocabulary, it is helpful to contrast passive vocabulary (*Yes, I've seen that word before and have a vague idea of what it means*) with active vocabulary (*Yes, I know that word and frequently use it when speaking and writing*). All of us have much larger passive lexicons that we draw upon when we read and listen to texts than active lexicons that we call into action when we speak and write. Knowing individual words and comprehending words in context are complicated by the fact that each discipline has its own lexicon or jargon and that an individual word might have a general meaning as well as a discipline-specific meaning. For example, students may know and use the word *capital* with its general meaning and not know the meaning of *capital* as used in business, or students may know the general meaning of *idealism* but not the meaning attached to the word in philosophy.

As well as linguistic knowledge, individuals need an internal system of pragmatic knowledge or communicative knowledge. Individuals with pragmatic knowledge know how to accomplish something with words (e.g.

greet someone, ask for information, ask for an extension on an assignment) and how to use language appropriately, taking into account the social context. For example, individuals know how to be polite and understand that politeness varies depending upon the social situation and upon whom one is talking to. Politely declining an invitation from a professor is done differently from declining an invitation from a classmate or close friend. Individuals with communicative knowledge understand different levels of formality and register, and this understanding impacts their speaking and writing as well as reading and listening comprehension. For example, following a class discussion or understanding a professor's side comments or jokes often requires pragmatic knowledge. When is someone being sarcastic, ironic or funny? Which statements are literal and which ones aren't? Pragmatic knowledge is sociocultural and allows individuals to recognize and use appropriate language in social situations. It seems most important in conversations yet comes into play in writing and comprehension also.

However, having adequate language proficiency and pragmatic knowledge does not ensure academic success. An important consideration, especially in reading and listening, is background knowledge or schema. Background or prior knowledge is culture-specific and influences reading and listening comprehension. For example, texts based on one's own culture are easier to read and understand than those based on someone else's culture (Carrell, 1983). Speaking and writing about a familiar topic is easier than speaking and writing about an unfamiliar one (Long, 1989; Schmidt-Rinehart, 1994). Language users bring their own set of cultural and social beliefs, experiences and assumptions to the text, whether it be written or spoken. McCormick *et al.* (1987: 9) state, 'Reading has both cognitive and cultural dimensions.' What type of prior knowledge do students bring to tasks? Carrell (1983) distinguishes between three types of knowledge: (a) linguistic knowledge; (b) content knowledge (knowledge about the topic); and (c) formal knowledge (knowledge of rhetorical styles, organizational patterns and interrelationships among items in a text). Students must be able to connect the new information they are receiving with their existing information, experience and beliefs. For example, a US history lecture may cover the post-World War II years and discuss the era of McCarthyism and the House Committee on Un-American Activities. Multilingual students, and even some US native English speakers, may have little content knowledge about this period in US history and have little understanding of the negative connotations the word *communism* carried and, for some people, still carries. Thus, students may lack sufficient content knowledge and a context to help them understand the lecture completely. Also, students may lack formal knowledge, knowledge of the organization and rhetorical style of the lecture. They may miss the organizational cues the professor gives such as 'Today we will discuss the effect this committee had ...' and be unable to decide what is important and what is less important; for example, a cue such as 'An interesting recent movie that deals with this period is *Good Night and Good Luck*. I recommend it', could either be a suggestion that the students should watch the movie or simply an aside.

Ultimately, all these types of knowledge (linguistic, pragmatic and background) are components of academic literacy and are essential components of thinking critically: comprehending, evaluating, analyzing and synthesizing material, and articulating and supporting an opinion effectively.

Common Groupings of Individual Skills

In thinking about language proficiency, we typically think of four major language skills: listening, speaking, reading and writing. Indeed, it is common, for faculty and for students, to note that a particular individual is better in one skill than the other skills. In reality, however, these skills are interrelated. Despite their interconnectedness and because of their individual qualities, two types of groupings are common for these skills. Perhaps the most common grouping of these four skills is into the two categories: (a) literacy skills (reading and writing); and (b) oracy or aural/oral skills (listening and speaking). In fact, English as a Second Language courses are often structured this way, with a reading/writing course and a separate listening/speaking course. Additionally, college composition courses emphasize reading and the incorporation and synthesis of academic texts into written work. At many institutions, there is a separate public speaking course, though this trend may be changing as more combined writing and speaking courses are being offered at the university level. Indeed, to be considered educated one must possess good literacy and oracy skills.

Another common grouping uses two different categories: (a) receptive skills (listening and reading), skills where there is no product or work created, where comprehension is key; and (b) productive skills (speaking and writing), skills where there is a product created (e.g. a speech or written passage). The receptive versus productive skills dichotomy is an old one. The receptive skills of listening and reading were traditionally thought of as passive skills under the assumption that individuals did not have to do much to listen or read; they could just sit back and take in the information. Hirvela (2004) points out that before the late 1980s 'reading was generally conceptualized as a passive act of *decoding meaning and information* in accordance with the intentions of the author of a text' (Hirvela, 2004: 9). Today researchers and language educators (e.g. Carrell, 1990; Eskey & Grabe, 1988; Reid, 1993) recognize that individuals play an active, even interactive, role when listening and reading. For example, to listen and understand, an individual must pay close attention, constantly checking and rechecking hypotheses and assumptions and tying in what is being said with the knowledge and experience one has. In short, individuals must make sense of the information they read or hear in relation to what they already know, thus drawing upon their background knowledge. They must negotiate meaning, interacting either literally or figuratively, with the speaker or writer of the text. Today the terms *active listening, negotiation of meaning* and *making meaning* are often used when talking about reading and listening. Just as reading and listening have traditionally been considered passive or receptive skills, writing and speaking have traditionally been considered productive ones. Individuals write an academic essay or deliver a well-argued persuasive speech. That is, they produce a product – a written or spoken work. Each of these groupings has its advantages and its limitations and is helpful in grasping what is involved in using language.

In the abstract, we can discuss language skills needed for success, assuming that individuals are tapping into their full linguistic and mental competence and knowledge (the cognitive aspects of language) and are in an optimal social situation (the socially-oriented aspects of language), yet, this may often not be true. Cognitively and socially, students in our class may not be in an ideal situation to do 'their best'. First, students must be open, willing and even eager to learn; in other words, they must be primed to learn and motivated. Second, internal and external distractions must be at a minimum. Internal distractions or impediments to comprehension include such things as having physical and/or mental health issues, not being alert and feeling marginalized or different from others. Physical and mental health issues include having a headache or a cold, being depressed or overly stressed, having a learning disability, being shy or uncomfortable with others in the group, fearing loss of face or being ridiculed if one speaks up in a discussion, and taking medications or illicit drugs. To be alert one must be rested, well fed, physically comfortable (or at least not very uncomfortable) and able to focus on the tasks at hand, which means putting aside other concerns for the time being. Nagging concerns might include financial problems, relationships, family obligations and work issues. External impediments to comprehension and skillful use of language include such things as the environment and the clarity and audibility of the delivery of the material. Environmental considerations include room temperature, ambient noise level, lighting, comfort of the seats, proximity of other students and acoustics. Clarity and audibility of the delivery of the material means that students can hear the speaker, can understand the pronunciation of the speaker, can see the speaker or visuals, and can decipher any printed material. In sum, a multitude of factors affect students' ability to benefit from our classes, learn new knowledge and skills, and connect new and old knowledge. Keeping this fact in mind, we understand that factors other than linguistic ability and intellectual ability are at play in academic success.

Much of the practical advice offered in this introductory chapter runs across the four basic language skills, emphasizing the interconnectedness of all four linguistic skills, each as part of a whole. The advice also cuts across disciplines. Faculty may intuitively implement classroom practices that assist students from diverse cultural, linguistic and educational backgrounds in learning and becoming scholars in their chosen disciplines. In the following four chapters, we address the four basic language skills: Speaking, Listening, Reading and Writing. In each chapter, we discuss each skill, provide a table listing common academic tasks that students are asked to do and the language skills involved, and also offer practical advice for helping students successfully accomplish the academic tasks presented. All academic tasks, of course, involve critical thinking skills to varying degrees as well as linguistic knowledge, pragmatic knowledge, and content and formal background knowledge. Our tips are not meant to be exhaustive but rather are meant to help faculty gain an understanding of the challenges multilingual students face, reflect upon their own teaching and develop strategies to assist all students in their disciplines and academic contexts.

3 Speaking

This is a very interesting picture of my evening class. On Wednesday night each week, there are almost twenty Asian students and five Americans sitting together in a room. The American students occupy the middle area of the room because it is the best place to raise their hands so that the teacher can call their names easily, while most Asian students hide in the corners of the room and stay at their seats to wait for the beginning of the class. We all know the US teaching style is learner-centered rather than teacher-centered, so the professor enjoys posing questions to us and hopes the students will discuss these topics positively. When it comes to answering questions, most Asian students have their heads down and keep silent. Sometimes, I feel the horrible silent atmosphere spread throughout the room. At this time, the Americans break the silence. Surprisingly, we Asian students can take a deep breath because the teacher will not call our names, and those American students will keep talking for a long time. At the end of class, the teacher still encourages us to express our ideas without concerns. The reason why I keep silent in the class is that I am afraid of my English and some stupid questions. But, I believe it will take time to become accustomed to the US classroom culture.

Graduate student from the People's Republic of China

The scene described above is familiar to faculty who teach classes with multilingual students, especially international students. Often, despite our desire to involve all students in class discussions, we may find that multilingual students generally participate less, letting American students carry the discussions. In addition to participating in class, students in universities are expected to successfully perform a wide variety of academic speaking tasks, ranging from making formal presentations to speaking to a professor outside of class. As the student above notes, students are judged whenever they speak, whether giving a graded speech, participating in class or asking an informational question after class. Faculty often complain to us about the inability of students to carry on a simple, in their estimation, conversation or answer a question. Frequently, faculty also comment on multilingual students' general unwillingness to communicate. Table 3.1 illustrates that academic speaking tasks actually (a) involve multiple language skills; and (b) require much of students. This is true whether the tasks are formal, semiformal or informal. In addition to linguistic skills, social and psychological factors contribute to students' success in undertaking and performing academic speaking tasks. These factors include communication apprehension, anxiety, motivation, self-confidence, alienation and introversion (Liu & Jackson, 2008). Keeping in mind the complexity and multilayered aspects of academic speaking tasks, we examine each type of task individually and offer practical advice.

Table 3.1 Academic speaking tasks and the language skills involved

Formal presentations	Semi-formal tasks	Informal tasks
Examples: speeches, debates, leading discussions, presentations	Examples: participation in class, small group discussion/work in and out of class	Examples: interactions with peers and faculty in person or on the phone
Listening – (a) understanding arguments, comments and questions from others; (b) understanding others' accents and speech patterns; (c) understanding speakers' opinions, attitudes and purpose. **Reading** – (a) comprehending material in preparation for speaking; (b) synthesizing information from numerous sources. **Speaking** – (a) delivery of prepared material with a focus on the components of delivery, content and organization; (b) responding to others' comments, arguments and questions; (c) summarizing others' comments and asking questions; (d) understanding the etiquette of turn-taking and other pragmatics of the situation. **Writing** – (a) planning and making notes, an outline, questions and supporting visuals; (b) composing and designing handouts.	**Listening** – (a) understanding content, questions and flow of a discussion in real time; (b) understanding others' accents and speech patterns; (c) understanding speakers' opinions, attitudes and purpose; (d) determining what is relevant and what isn't. **Reading** – comprehending material in preparation for speaking. (*Students may perceive this as nonessential and not do it.*) **Speaking** – (a) voicing ideas and opinions; (b) asking and answering questions spontaneously; (c) understanding the etiquette of turn-taking and other pragmatics of the situation; (d) agreeing and disagreeing respectfully. **Writing** – (a) taking notes on the discussion; (b) completing an assigned writing task. (*Students may perceive this as nonessential and not do it.*)	**Listening** – (a) understanding content, questions and flow of a discussion in real time; (b) understanding others' accents and speech patterns; (c) understanding speakers' opinions, attitudes and purpose; (d) determining what is relevant and what isn't. **Reading** – comprehending material in preparation for conversation. (*There may actually be little or no reading that is required prior to or during the encounters.*) **Speaking** – (a) voicing ideas, (b) asking and responding to questions and comments spontaneously; (c) understanding the etiquette of turn-taking and other pragmatics of the situation; (d) agreeing and disagreeing respectfully. **Writing** – (a) making notes in preparation for the interaction; (b) taking notes during the interaction.

Formal Academic Speaking Tasks

Formal speaking tasks, such as making a speech, participating in a debate, leading a discussion or making a presentation, require preparation that generally involves reading and writing and may involve listening. Formal academic speaking tasks may be easier for students than less formal ones because students have time to plan and rehearse these presentations beforehand; that is, they have more control. However, in formal academic speaking tasks more emphasis is placed on delivery and components such as pronunciation, volume, pacing, posture and eye contact. Additionally, stress and anxiety levels are high for most students in these formal situations; this seems especially true for those who feel their overall language skills are not as good as their peers' as well as for those who have had little experience speaking in public. Here are a few practical tips to help multilingual students, and all students, be more successful with the formal academic speaking tasks listed in column one of Table 3.1.

Practical tips to help students with formal academic speaking tasks

(1) Be aware of anxiety inherent in public speaking, often more pronounced in multilingual students. Acknowledge that most people are nervous and this 'condition' is not easily overcome. Instead, consider discussing strategies for dealing with anxiety and using it to one's benefit. For example, encourage students to choose topics that are familiar, focus on communicating with the audience as if in a conversation and practice repeatedly.

(2) Provide students with explicit instructions for assignments.

(a) Give students guidelines for choosing a topic or assign topics. Help students in choosing and researching their topics by providing advice on where to find information and indicating what type of resources are acceptable (e.g. can students use *Wikipedia*, blogs, popular magazines?). Approve all topics and do not allow students to deliver a speech, lead a discussion or hold a debate on a topic you have not approved. Don't hesitate to say why a particular topic does not meet the requirements of the assignment.

(b) If it is a group presentation or debate, make it clear what you expect. For example, should each person speak or can one person prepare the graphics and not assist with delivery of the debate or presentation? Group presentations and projects can be tricky to implement and execute successfully. Because group presentations and other projects are common today and are different than individual assignments, we devote a chapter to the topic of group work: Chapter 7: Working in Groups.

(c) Use rubrics or other guidelines for formal presentations; in other words, make assessment criteria explicit. (See the appendix for sample rubrics and other evaluation tools.) Guidelines help students prepare their presentations, know what is expected and understand how they will be evaluated. Typically, rubrics for formal speeches contain information about content, organization, delivery and allotted time. If it is a group presentation, guidelines may also include how each person's contribution and performance is evaluated.

(3) Provide students with models of successful, and even not so successful, presentations when possible. After obtaining permission from past students, make their speeches available to students to watch outside of class or, if time permits, watch and critique them in class together, using the rubric for the assignment if one was given. The examples need not be perfect. A discussion of the strengths and weaknesses of each speech can be very helpful to students. Features to discuss can include delivery, content, organization and overall effectiveness.

(4) Use speeches and presentations given by professionals in the discipline as models of how to and how not to deliver speeches. Again, if time permits, a class discussion of the strengths and weaknesses (e.g. delivery, content, organization and overall effectiveness) can be helpful; if time does not permit this in-class analysis, have students critique the speeches outside of class. Websites such as americanrhetoric.com are good resources for well-known speeches.

(5) Expose students to speakers with different accents through student models and professional speeches. Research (e.g. Flowerdew, 1994) shows that individuals who are exposed to a variety of accents become accustomed to different accents and can more easily comprehend accented speech than individuals who have had little exposure to accents different from their own. The distinction between *accent* and *pronunciation* is important to understand, especially in today's global environment. *Accent* is a pattern of pronunciation, typically associated with a region, ethnicity or class, whereas *pronunciation* is the articulation of particular words; information regarding pronunciation is given in dictionaries in the International Phonetic Alphabet (IPA) or other transcription system. Accent, on the other hand, is personal and may be tied to an individual's identity.

(6) Encourage students to look up the pronunciation of key words and proper nouns for their presentations. The goal in speaking is effective

communication, so intelligibility is paramount – a native-like accent is not. Regardless of accent, speakers need to pronounce words correctly, especially proper nouns (e.g. names, places) and key words and phrases. By checking online, in dictionaries and/or with other individuals before their presentations, students can learn to pronounce important words correctly.

(7)   Encourage students to practice their speeches ahead of time by going to a speaking center on campus and/or recording and then listening to their practice speech. Students can use an MP3 program such as Audacity to record and play back their presentation. It may also be possible for students to videotape themselves and watch and critique their practice performance.

(8)   Have pre-presentation check-ins with classmates and/or faculty when possible. For example, consider having students submit an outline for their formal presentation and a list of references in the documentation style of the discipline. These can be submitted prior to the presentation for faculty or peer review and feedback. Another possible check-in time is during a class period when, individually or in small groups, students give short progress reports on their upcoming presentations. Check-ins hold students accountable for working on their presentations and make it harder for students to put everything off until the last minute. In addition, these check-ins can assist students with the process in that peers can often provide valuable feedback and suggestions. Additionally, the peer reviewer as well as the peer presenter benefit from the process. Consider giving points for these in-progress reports.

(9)   Hold students responsible for the directions given. Hold students to deadlines and the requirements of the assignment. For instance, be strict about time limits for presentations. Faculty may wish to give a range of time allotted for speeches (e.g. a 6–8 minute speech or a 10–12 minute one). Even when indicating a range, train students to pay attention and use their time wisely. You may wish to have another student be the timekeeper, using a timer and cards to hold up as the time progresses (e.g. five minutes, two minutes, one minute). Consider lowering the grade if presentations are not within the prescribed time frame (i.e. too short or too long) or if they do not follow other requirements such as documenting sources.

(10) Encourage students to draw upon their individual knowledge, experience and interests in choosing topics, doing the research and making presentations. Help multilingual students understand that

their language abilities and experiences are assets. Two cases where multilingual students might draw on their experiences when presenting are (a) using practices or experiences in another country or culture as examples to make a point, draw an analogy or provide evidence; or (b) using non-English words to explain a concept or idea that is not easily expressed in English. For example, in discussing how suffering is viewed and handled by different cultures, a student of Japanese heritage or with familiarity with Japanese culture might explain the word *gaman*, defined as 'enduring the seemingly unbearable with patience and dignity' (Hirasuna, 2005) or use the newly created Japanese word *karoshi*, meaning 'exhaustion death' to explain differences in work ethics. In explaining concepts such as *gaman* and *karoshi* in English and then using the Japanese words, students can draw from their experiences with Japan and/or Japanese culture, thus offering a fresh perspective on the issues of suffering and work. Another example is the use of the German world *umwelt* by animal behaviorists. According to Yoon (2009), *umwelt* literally means 'the environment' or 'the world around', but animal behaviorists use it to evoke the perceived world view of an individual species, 'the world sensed by an animal, a view idiosyncratic to each species, fueled by its particular sensory and cognitive powers and limited by its deficits' (Yoon, 2009: 15). In giving a presentation on animal behavior, a student may wish to explain in English and use the German word *umwelt* to capture a concept for which English doesn't have a word. Certainly, any student can use words from other languages to help explain a concept (e.g. *gestalt*), but often multilingual students may erroneously think they can't use a non-English word when giving a speech in English. We can dissuade them of this belief and help them see their knowledge of other languages and cultures is an asset.

(11) Promote peer respect. Discuss the importance of the audience being supportive and attentive, explaining that listeners must share the responsibility for comprehension. Listeners have an active role to play in communication. In 'Chapter 4: Listening', we offer advice for helping students become active, responsible listeners.

(12) Provide students with feedback on their formal presentations. This can be done in a number of different ways and need not be time consuming.

    (a) If you used a rubric, then make comments following it. Make suggestions for improvement, giving students specific things that they can do to improve their content, organization and delivery.

    (b) Have students evaluate classmates' presentations and/or ask questions. This can benefit the speakers as well as the listeners and underscores the fact that communication takes both listener and speaker. (See the appendix for sample peer evaluation forms.)

    (c) Provide feedback as soon as possible after a presentation, but do not interrupt the student while he is speaking. Jot down comments during each individual presentation. Also, collect examples and points that will be helpful to everyone, such as tips about eye contact and/or posture, about structuring an introduction, about adding details, about controlling nervousness, and about the pronunciation of word endings. (A common mistake is not pronouncing word endings such as 'ed', 's' and 'ing'). If the presentations are videotaped and time allows, review the videotape to add to your critique.

(13) Help students take responsibility for improving their performances and overall speaking abilities.

    (a) Encourage or require self-evaluations of formal presentations, both individual and group. This can be done by having presentations videotaped and made available to students to view and evaluate using a list of provided questions. A self-evaluation sheet with a few general questions can be completed after the presentation or after viewing the presentation. (See the appendix for sample self-evaluation forms.)

    (b) Encourage students to work to improve their overall fluency and accuracy in speaking on their own. Accuracy refers to grammatical correctness whereas fluency refers to one's ability to speak easily and be understood. Therefore, a student can be fluent but make numerous grammatical errors, often ones that don't impede comprehension. On the other hand, a student can speak very carefully and accurately, but the conversation can seem choppy or even disjointed. Students overly concerned with accuracy may seldom speak and when they do, may speak slowly and seem ill at ease. Students can build both fluency and accuracy by practicing both formal and informal presentations, by recording themselves and then reviewing and critiquing the recordings. Also, students can practice reading aloud, recording themselves, and reviewing their MP3 files. Simply reading English aloud can improve their fluency and make them more comfortable speaking English. Many public speaking instructors include reading a passage aloud as an initial, often ungraded, speech assignment to help put students at ease and work on their delivery. Students can also listen to a portion of a book-on-tape, make a recording of the same section, and review and compare their voice to that of the professional reader.

(c) Encourage students to take advantage of on-campus programs and resources. Many campuses have a speaking center where students can receive assistance with oral presentations. Universities may have conversation partner programs, language exchange programs or buddy systems in which students can be matched with other students. There are also student clubs and organizations that provide ways for students to get involved in the university, meet new people and, in the process, practice their English conversation skills. These are simple suggestions to make to students, especially to those who seem to be struggling or to be uncomfortable speaking English and to those who ask for advice on improving their overall speaking skills.

Semi-Formal Academic Speaking Tasks

Participation in class and in groups is generally considered important in US classrooms, yet asking and responding to questions and actively joining in discussions are not simple tasks, as indicated in the second column in Table 3.1 and as expressed by the graduate student at the beginning of this chapter. Participating in class discussions and in peer groups, inside and outside of class, is more spontaneous than formal speaking tasks but also involves linguistic, pragmatic and background knowledge as do formal tasks. (Here we are using group work as two or more students working together on an assignment, so it includes pair work.)

Certainly reading assigned material and taking notes or writing responses in preparation for class are helpful for in-class participation, even though students may not view this work as a priority or as essential. With out-of-class group projects, reading and writing play a larger role than they do for in-class discussions and group work. With out-of-class projects, students generally are required to do research (i.e. reading, summarizing, analyzing and synthesizing material) as well as produce a final product (i.e. a written group report, oral presentation or both). In all of these semi-formal activities, however, students must be good listeners. In order to contribute to class or group discussions, students must listen carefully. First, the speaker's words, phrases, sentences and overall discourse must be intelligible and comprehensible to the listener. However, simply comprehending what is said is generally not enough to actively participate in discussions.

Ideally, students have read material related to the topic of discussion. In short, listeners understand more if they have background knowledge, information about the content of the discussion. On top of this, they need to understand the 'rules of engagement'; that is, the etiquette of participating in a discussion: being familiar with turn-taking rules (e.g. when it's okay to interrupt, how to hold the floor) and other pragmatic and cultural rules (e.g. how to ask informational questions as well as questions for clarification, how to politely disagree with others). Unlike formal academic speaking, participating in discussions must be done in real time with little or no planning. These semi-formal tasks require spontaneity, confidence and being able to think on your feet. These are difficult skills for all students, but especially for those who may feel unsure of their language skills and/or of their ideas. All students want to be perceived as articulate and intelligent, so they may hesitate to speak in public situations.

Additionally, in US classrooms student behavior is often different than in classrooms in other countries. For example, Huang and Brown (2009: 648) note 'Chinese students are not very active in answering teachers' questions or participating in classroom discussions.' They argue that this is not because Chinese students are shy or have nothing to say, but rather it is because they care deeply about what others, faculty and peers, think about them. They are often afraid of making mistakes, not answering a simple question correctly or saying something others will consider foolish. *Face*, a positive presentation of self, is very important in Asian cultures, so students do not wish to lose face or be embarrassed. This seems true of the student's description of her class that opens this chapter and of most students, in fact. We want others to think highly of us. A Chinese student told us that in China students become anxious when the teacher asks questions, few students raise their hands to answer questions, and if a student gives an incorrect answer, he often feels he has lost face and disappointed the instructor. In fact, the student may have to meet with the instructor after class to review the material. This often causes students to feel ashamed. These examples underscore the fact that cultures, experiences, traditions and values influence classroom behavior and learning.

In addition to cultural and educational experiences and values, personal characteristics (e.g. individual shyness) and classroom or group dynamics (e.g. certain students dominating conversations) influence students' participation. Vandrick (2003: 2) notes that 'Many students simply do not feel "entitled" to participate'; they do not feel they have 'power' and, therefore, silence themselves. Vandrick argues that gender and social class as well as linguistic confidence and cultural and educational background influence students' feelings of entitlement to speak. Gender also affects participation; research of student behavior in Western classrooms shows that females tend to speak less and to receive less attention than males (e.g. Jule, 2004; Sadker & Sadker, 1994; Spender, 1980). All these variables interact and intersect in complicated ways. Being aware of them and the complexity of their interaction can inform us and our classroom practices.

We are not arguing that participation should not be encouraged or expected. Indeed, to succeed in academe as well as the professional world, students need to develop effective speaking skills and become somewhat at ease participating in large and small groups. How can faculty assist students in becoming comfortable and effective doing so? Here are a few practical pieces of advice.

Practical tips to help students with semi-formal academic speaking tasks

(1) Be aware that multilingual students may find it difficult to speak in class for a variety of reasons and that they may not feel entitled to speak up and be heard. Help them understand that they can speak up and that their views are valued.

(2) Explain clearly what participation means in the typical US classroom and what it means in your class, as well as why participation is considered important. If time allows, discuss cultural differences in classroom behavior and expectations without identifying one cultural practice as better than another. Many international students come from cultures where classes are mainly lecture-style or teacher-centered, not the learner-centered classroom where students are expected to actively participate.

(3) Define participation broadly so that it includes signs of attentiveness, engagement and interest, not just speaking in class. Notice students' body language (e.g. nodding their heads, maintaining eye contact, leaning forward) and general preparedness for class (Vandrick, 2003).

(4) Set the tone and environment for respectful discussions and interactions between students and faculty and among students. This can be done by including statements on the course syllabi that state explicitly that all discussions will be respectful, that all views are valued, and that discussions can be heated, but not personal. By modeling respectful and equal treatment of students and by not tolerating inappropriate speech (e.g. racist, homophobic, sexist, xenophobic), faculty send signals of what is and is not acceptable.

(5) Whenever possible, give students some time to think and plan before they have to speak. Faculty can provide students with discussion questions through posts, discussion boards, handouts or blogs before the class so that students have time to formulate opinions and ideas. If discussion questions are not provided ahead of time, there are several ways faculty can give students 'thinking' time in class. One way is to announce the discussion questions and then give students a few minutes to jot down their ideas before beginning the class discussion. Another possibility is to have students discuss questions, problems or issues with one or two other students before beginning the whole class discussion. If small groups talk about the questions prior to a whole class discussion, each group can briefly report on their conversation to start the whole class discussion. This procedure holds each group accountable for their discussion. Small groups can be assigned different discussion questions or problems. In the same way, individuals can be assigned specific questions, given time to plan their responses, and then give their comments to their small group or to the whole class.

(6) Provide opportunities for small group discussions in and out of class. Students generally feel more comfortable talking in a small group than in a larger group. Speaking in small groups provides practice, and can be a rehearsal for a large group discussion. Small group or pair work can also be used for rehearsing formal presentations and debates. Again, these provide students with practice and allow them to get feedback from peers. If groups are used for rehearsal, each member can complete a peer evaluation form for another member. In peer evaluation, students can give their comments orally as well as in writing.

(7) Encourage all students to participate in class discussions. Participation not only helps students learn the course content, but it also helps students improve their speaking skills, practice the pragmatics of conversing, and gain confidence in expressing themselves. Here are some suggestions on how to incorporate participation:

(a) If the class is relatively small, try to get everyone to speak. However, randomly calling on students can produce anxiety, especially early in the semester when students do not know their classmates or feel comfortable speaking to the whole class. On the other hand, calling on individual students in a systematic way (e.g. by going around the room and calling on each person or going down the class roster) can lead to students not paying attention after they have spoken. At the same time, calling on students in a systematic way may relieve some of the stress as students can plan ahead.

(b) If faculty know a student has particular knowledge about a subject or interest in a specific subject, they can ask that student questions related to his knowledge and interest. Knowing about a subject allows the student to be more comfortable speaking as the content is familiar. Additionally, it allows him to contribute to class and be seen as knowledgeable or expert on a topic. A word of caution is in order, however. Avoid asking students questions that put them in a position to speak for a whole culture, country, race or gender. In other words avoid stereotypes. Don't assume that because a student looks Chinese that he can explain Confucianism or that a Hispanic student can answer a question about drug cartels in Mexico today. In other words, avoid essentializing students or assuming that members of a specific ethnic or linguistic group share most characteristics.

(8) Base a percentage of the course grade on participation if that is valued in a course. Make it clear to students how much participation counts in their grade. Participating in class is often a new experience for multi-lingual students as their educational backgrounds have been more teacher-centered and examination-driven than is common in Western universities. Remember that multilingual students may be concerned about losing face and making mistakes in front of others. Moreover, the concept of students having something worthwhile to contribute in class is new for some students and speaking up in class, especially a large class, can be frightening. Even fluent English speakers may be nervous, worried about sounding unintelligent, or afraid of being misunderstood. The logistics of keeping track of an individual student's contributions in class may seem taxing and often faculty do so holistically, quickly getting a sense of who speaks up and who is more reticent, whose contributions move the discussion forward and whose add little. Faculty can keep track of student participation more systematically, however. For example, instructors can keep a tally of the number of times students speak in class and give full points to those who participate most. If faculty wish to also include an evaluative component, they can give a √+ (excellent), √ (good) or √- (weak) for each contribution with each category carrying a different number of points, for example, 3, 2 and 1 respectively. A business faculty member explained her systematic method: she keeps a tally of who contributes a comment or question in class. At the beginning of the semester, she makes a spreadsheet with all the students' names and a column for each class meeting. She tells students they must speak at least twice each session to get full credit for

participation, which is a certain percentage of the final grade. She makes a check mark by each student's name when he contributes to class discussion. Students get credit, a check mark, each time they speak. Their comments are not evaluated for content. By encouraging students to participate in class, whether faculty keep track systematically or holistically, students begin to feel more comfortable speaking up. Students can practice and build on their success.

(9) Help students become strategic about participating in class. If participation is important, suggest that students consciously try to ask a question or make a comment at least once in each class. Students can prepare one or two questions and comments about the material to be covered and then during class or group discussion make themselves speak up.

Informal Academic Speaking Tasks

Informal speaking tasks in academic settings, outlined in column three of Table 3.1, are even more spontaneous than formal and semi-formal academic speaking tasks, yet they may cause as much or more apprehension and anxiety for the student as in-class activities. In these interactions, success depends not only upon linguistic skills but also on pragmatic and background knowledge. Outside-of-class interactions between faculty and students and among students are important because they provide opportunities for students to master content material and make connections with faculty, students and others. These outside-of-class informal interactions also give those involved an impression of a student's overall language abilities and grasp of the subject material. Indeed, when professors contact us about a multilingual student's difficulty in class, they often cite the fact that the student cannot follow and participate in a simple conversation with them or their classmates. Multilingual students' nervousness in outside-of-class interactions may be rooted in a lack of confidence in their cultural (i.e. pragmatic) as well as linguistic abilities. What is polite in the US may be considered rude in another culture and/or country. Multilingual students may feel they are being very polite when, in fact, a Westerner would consider them rude. For instance, when our office doors are open, we have had international students from China enter our offices, walk around our desks and stand very close to us to ask a question, thereby invading what we consider our 'personal space'. Another time a student wished to thank a faculty member for her assistance and approached her with arms outstretched, ready to give her a hug. A science faculty member reported that she received emails from international students with closings of 'I love you'. In these instances, students seem unaware of how their actions and statements appear to others. Faculty can help students by politely informing them when their actions or statements can be perceived as rude or inappropriate and suggest culturally appropriate comments and behaviors. Simple statements like 'You should know that hugging a professor or signing an email to a professor with "I love you" is inappropriate because those actions are too personal. I know you didn't mean to be rude, but your actions may be perceived that way.' Then faculty can continue by offering examples of common closings and statements to show gratitude. We have found that students are appreciative of being told their actions or statements are considered rude because actually they had often thought they were being polite, expressing their gratitude.

Another practice that seems to be more common among multilingual students than among native English speakers is bringing a friend or relative to meetings with faculty. This may not cause problems in many cases, but in others it may. For example, students may bring someone to serve as a translator, thereby letting the friend do most of the talking, and the person may even translate the conversation for the student. In such a situation, it is difficult for faculty to know what the student understands, what difficulties he is having and how to assist the student. The practice of visiting a faculty member in a small group may be common in students' home countries, or they may feel more comfortable having a friend or friends with them. This is often appropriate in the US also. Individual faculty must decide when it's appropriate for students to speak privately with them (e.g. about grades or other private matters) and when it's appropriate for students to meet with faculty as a small group (e.g. asking for clarification about an assignment, asking questions about the course material). As much as possible, however, it seems best to avoid allowing others to serve as translators.

As faculty are generally not involved in informal interactions among students outside of class, they have limited control over such interactions. Setting a respectful, inclusive tone and environment in class can translate into more respectful interactions among students. Of course, faculty need to respond if students make discriminatory comments about other students based on their ethnicity or linguistic background (e.g. 'X can't speak English, so please don't put him in my group.' 'There are too many non-native English speakers in this class, and they slow the class down.') and deal with complaints about disrespectful or discriminatory behavior towards them by classmates or others. Faculty need to listen, offer advice and take action when necessary (i.e. situations of harassment or discrimination).

Less preparation by students is needed for informal interactions compared with what is required for formal and semi-formal academic speaking tasks. Preparations for informal interactions are often limited to jotting down questions to ask, which might include questions about reading material, the lectures or assignments. Once a student asks a question, however, the crucial skills are listening and responding in real time. As with the semi-formal discussions and group activities, participating in a conversation is hard work in that one must be able to understand the accent and speech patterns of the speaker (e.g. differences in dialect); understand the words, phrases, and sentences; understand the inferences and implications that indicate the speaker's attitudes and intentions; as well as determine what is relevant and what is irrelevant. Understanding must be followed by responding in an appropriate respectful manner, which means adhering to the etiquette of turn-taking, abiding by rules of behavior (e.g. valuing personal space, addressing individuals respectfully), asking and responding to questions and comments spontaneously, and agreeing and disagreeing respectfully. Skills in reading and writing play a minor role in being successful in informal speaking activities. For example, students may reread material in preparation for a meeting and during the conversation make notes on important information. Even though these informal interactions are unscripted, there are things faculty can do to make them more successful and satisfying for all parties. Here are a few pieces of advice:

Practical tips to help students with informal academic speaking tasks

(1) Make students as comfortable as possible when they speak to you individually. Multilingual students are often not used to approaching authority figures such as professors. They may also be hesitant to ask those in authority questions, fearing that their questions may make them look foolish or that they may be wasting the professor's time. Practice patience giving them time to speak. Reword their questions, their responses to questions, and your advice or instructions. In sum, before they leave be sure they understand and have the needed information.

(2) Offer students simple things to do that seem obvious to faculty, including informing students of the resources on campus. For example, students may be unaware that they can make an appointment with a reference librarian to help them with their research, may not know that there is a writing and/or speaking center, or may not realize that

student tutors are available for certain courses. Besides not knowing what services are available on campus, students may not think of simpler things they can do to ease difficulties they are having. For example, a student may visit a faculty member to express difficulty in participating in class and ask for advice. In this case, it can be helpful to offer basic advice such as (a) look over the material to be covered in class ahead of time and write down two or three comments and two or three questions; (b) make yourself contribute at least twice during each class discussion and more than three times in small group discussions. Actually count the number of times you contribute to the class discussions. Set goals and keep track of how many times you speak up; (c) form a study group with classmates so you can discuss the material and become more familiar with it and comfortable talking about it. Again, bring prepared questions and comments to the study group; and (d) try to move the discussion forward with your comments when participating in class and in small groups. You have a unique perspective so can help others see issues differently. In sum, faculty can state the simple and obvious. Even if students have thought of these things or are doing them, hearing them again and from an authority figure is important and helpful.

(3) Try to focus on the content of what students say and not the way it is said. Students are often unfamiliar with how to make polite requests, ask questions or make comments in an academic context. Unintentionally, they may be perceived as rude but in actuality they may simply not know the 'rules of etiquette' or the pragmatics of the situation. A student who blurts out in class 'That's wrong. The XYZ organization lies' may simply not know how to politely disagree. A student who asks 'Have you finished grading our exams yet? You've had a week' may not realize how accusatory faculty may find the question and statement. In both cases, faculty can point out to the individual privately more civil ways to disagree or ask such questions. Of course, sometimes students know the linguistic rules of etiquette and choose to ignore them. Determining the intentionality of students' actions can be difficult.

(4) When responding to a student request, avoid nuanced answers as much as possible. Choose to say things directly instead of by implication or inference. For example, if a student asks to submit a paper late for a specific reason, explain the policy clearly. 'I do not accept late papers' or 'You may have a few extra days to work on your paper. Your paper will be counted down one letter grade for each day it is late and I will not accept it after X day.'

Students may make requests that are difficult for faculty to understand. They are often under tremendous internal and external pressure from family. They may be the first in their family to go to college. Their family may be making monetary and other types of sacrifices for them to attend college. Parents, especially of international students, may have chosen their major, expecting them to do well and then take over the family business. International students, especially those of privilege, may also be used to negotiating and pushing for what they want or may have had others, such as parents, who solved problems for them. In other words, they may not understand the differences in the acceptable behavior in a Western academic context. Some may have trouble accepting an answer they don't like. A student may request that the grade on a particular assignment or even in a course be changed. Reasons may or may not be legitimate, including 'If I don't get a good grade in your class, I will be kicked out of school/I will lose my scholarship.' 'My parents have paid a lot of money, and you are the only one who can help me stay in school.' After listening to the student's reasons, the faculty member can make a decision on the spot or can tell the student that he will gather more information, consider the request and get back to him. It is best, whenever possible, to tell a student the answer as soon as possible and avoid raising his hopes. If told an answer they don't like, students often keep repeating their request, adding no new information. They may come back to a faculty member's office repeatedly asking the same questions. They may solicit others to support their case, perhaps even bringing a friend or relative with them to again reiterate their request. Simply acknowledge their feelings and request, and then repeat your answer. There's no need to elaborate. If there is an appeal process (e.g. to appeal a course grade), then the faculty should inform the student and explain the procedure.

4 Listening

I kept listening. But I couldn't understand very much, and my notes a mess. A lot of words and no meaning. Later I realized that this professor, he likes to tell jokes and stories in the middle of his lecture.
Student from Poland (cited in Gebhard, 2010: 13)

I grew up hearing British English spoken with an Indian accent. I was very surprised when I could not understand the American accent. I have to listen carefully.
Student from India (cited in Gebhard, 2010: 14)

The first semester, I had difficulty understanding the lectures because the professors didn't follow the book. The second semester was better because the professors' lectures mostly followed the book so I could prepare for the lectures by reading the textbook.
Undergraduate student from Japan

We may view listening, like speaking, as a relatively simple and singular task – comprehending the spoken word. However, in reality it entails a complicated web of skills. The student comments above speak to the complexity of listening to lectures and conversations. In listening and reading, individuals must decode individual words and phrases; in other words, they process information from the bottom up. At the same time, individuals need to process information from the top down, to listen and read for overall meaning. Faculty have commented to us on the difficulty of measuring listening comprehension. How do we tell if students have understood what has been said? Typically, faculty make judgments about listening comprehension based on such things as students' spoken and written responses to questions ('I ask her a simple question, and she can't answer it.'), on students' questions ('She asked a question that I had just answered. Wasn't she listening?'), and on students' behavior ('My students give me these blank looks. They can't follow simple instructions.'). However, there can be problems at any point during the process of hearing spoken language and then producing some verbal or nonverbal response. Summarizing information, synthesizing new information with one's own background knowledge, and thinking critically are required to fully process the spoken word. Also, at times any student, multilingual or monolingual, for whatever reason, simply does not concentrate or pay attention. As can be seen in Table 4.1, listening, though at times called a passive skill, is not passive at all. To listen and fully understand oral language can be hard work, especially if one is unfamiliar with the vocabulary, content, pragmatics of the situation or rhetorical style.

Listening is closely related to reading in that both are comprehension tasks. Today's multimedia presentations, by faculty and peers, generally contain both oral and visual input, thereby calling upon listening and reading skills simultaneously. Indeed, faculty often use PowerPoint and other presentation software when lecturing so that students today may not commonly encounter formal lectures and other information delivery systems that have only oral input. Both listening and reading ask individuals to understand a written or spoken text, weave new information in with their existing knowledge, and make sense of the information.

Table 4.1 Academic listening tasks and the language skills involved

Formal listening tasks with and without multimedia	Understanding and following oral directions
Examples: lectures, panels, presentations, individual student and group presentations, videos, podcasts, multimedia presentations	Examples: directions for classroom activities, homework assignments, exams, procedures
Listening – (a) understanding speakers' accents and speech patterns; (b) understanding the individual words, content, organization and rhetorical style; (c) understanding speakers' attitudes and intentions; (d) integrating the incoming messages from different media (e.g. live speech and PowerPoint slides); (e) being able to concentrate for long stretches of time; (f) determining the relationships among ideas, what is relevant and what is not; (g) relating new information to background knowledge.	**Listening** – (a) understanding speakers' accents and speech patterns; (b) decoding individual words, phrases and sentences; (c) understanding the overall content; (d) tying in what is understood with individual background knowledge about types of assignments and tasks (i.e. formal background knowledge); (e) deciding what is important and what is not important; (f) understanding answers and comments given to questions.
Reading – (a) reading material in preparation (*Students may perceive this as nonessential and not do it*); (b) reading the texts in visuals (e.g. titles, headings, figures, statistics, outlines).	**Reading** – reading any written directions.
Speaking – (a) asking questions during and/or after the lecture; (b) participating in discussions on material as required.	**Speaking** – (a) asking questions for clarification and information; (b) rephrasing of instructions for verification of comprehension.
Writing – (a) taking notes on what is presented; (b) writing formal summaries, outlines, evaluations or answers to questions about content and speakers' attitudes and opinions. (*These may be assignments.*)	**Writing** – taking notes based on what is said and understood.

As can be seen in Table 4.1, we group academic listening tasks into two categories: (a) formal listening tasks, which may or may not include multimedia such as lectures, panels, presentations by faculty and students, videos, podcasts; and (b) understanding and following oral directions for such tasks as classroom activities, assignments, exams and procedures.

Formal Listening Tasks

In listening as in reading, especially in formal listening tasks, knowledge of vocabulary related to the subject matter and content background information are paramount. Formal background knowledge, the ability to recognize and anticipate common organizational and rhetorical patterns in a lecture and/or a written text, also greatly aids comprehension. With this formal knowledge, individuals fill in gaps, make and test their understanding, and do not have to rely strictly on linguistic knowledge and decoding skills. Cultural experiences and expectations also impact listening comprehension. For example, lecture styles in one country may be very different from styles in another country. Huang and Brown (2009) report research results that outline Chinese students' challenges understanding North American lecture styles, all of which stem from differences in student expectations and experiences. In China, faculty closely follow the textbook, allot little time to student participation and discussion, use the blackboard extensively, and provide a lecture summary at the end of each lecture. In the United States, academic lectures tend to be very different. Thus, Chinese students' expectations are not met, and they may have difficulty understanding the lectures. In fact, surveys of Chinese students studying in the United States reveal that Chinese students feel too much discussion, poor lecture organization, lack of detailed notes on the blackboard, and a lack of lecture summaries make it more difficult for them to comprehend academic lectures.

Students from other cultures and traditions may expect academic lectures to be organized differently than in China or the United States. Students' expectations about rhetorical style and organization of lectures influence their comprehension. Is a lecture in politics organized as a classification of political parties during a specific time period, in an economics lecture does the professor compare and contrast the present economic situation and the Great Depression, or in an engineering class does the professor present the relationship between experimental data and theory? Is there a main textbook that most lectures loosely follow?

To follow a lecture adequately, in addition to understanding how the lecture is organized, students need to recognize cues or markers that indicate what is important and what is not. Examples of such markers are 'One of the most important events was . . .' 'Next we'll discuss the implications of . . .' or 'Let me tell you an amusing story about the Democratic candidate'. The first two examples signal important information while the last one is an aside. These cues provide roadmaps in listening and reading comprehension – unaware of them, students may get lost. Of course, when reading a text, students can go back and reread, can look up words they are unsure about, can note headings and other textual cues, all of which are not available when listening to a live lecture. Even if the professor uses visuals to augment a live lecture, students do not have the time to look words up and cannot go back and review points during the lecture. If a lecture is filmed and put on the web or course software or even made into a podcast, students can look up words and concepts, review the lecture and replay it again and again.

It is also true that when listening, unlike when reading, an individual has no control over the pace (i.e. speed of delivery) or the accents and speech patterns of the speakers. In fact, two comments multilingual students frequently make are that accents and rates of speech make comprehension of the content of a lecture more difficult. Research suggests that individuals have more trouble comprehending unfamiliar accents than those with which they are more familiar (e.g. Flowerdew, 1994). In addition, Flowerdew (1994) suggests that native English speakers more easily understand a range of accents than non-native English speakers do. However, the reality is that students, as well as the rest of us, encounter a range of accents, both native and non-native. In today's world it seems impossible to only interact with individuals who speak with the same accent as we do. In fact, exposure to different accents is beneficial and prepares students for the world of work and the diverse world in which we live. Consistent exposure to different accents allows students to improve their comprehension. If we hear complaints from students about 'difficult' accents, we need to urge them to continue listening and assure them that their comprehension will improve. We can also suggest strategies for coming to class primed for the content and for being more active listeners.

Native English speakers also seem to fare better adjusting to different rates of speech than do multilingual students. Research suggests that rate of speech does not impact native English speakers' comprehension as much as it does the comprehension of international students (Flowerdew, 1994). Reasons for native English speakers dealing with accents and rate of speech better than international students may be that native English speakers can fill in the gaps better than international students can. That is, native

English speakers can obtain a maximum amount of information from the passage by using their overall knowledge of English 'to assign syntax and predict which words would be content words' (Flowerdew, 1994: 22). Several studies also suggest that native English speakers are better able to infer meaning whereas non-native English speakers rely more on decoding or understanding individual words. This may be due to the fact that native English speakers have more cultural and formal background knowledge, allowing them to fill in the gaps.

Unlike in the past, today's students may encounter multimedia presentations more frequently than situations where no visuals are used. However, delivery of information via audio media only still exists in podcasts, radio programs and live lectures and presentations without graphics. Many students seem to prefer visual learning though and benefit from several modes of input and, indeed, students today are generally accustomed to multimedia presentations. Visuals allow students to see important words and organizational cues, allowing them to follow the oral presentation. Additionally, students may recognize a word when it is written but not be familiar with its pronunciation. Visuals may also help focus students' attention and increase comprehension.

Listening comprehension, as a receptive skill, is hard to assess and measure. Additionally, it is hard to determine the reasons a student misunderstands. However, there are things faculty can do to help students be competent and active listeners.

Practical tips to help students with formal academic listening tasks

(1) Make the environment as conducive as possible for all students to hear and see optimally. If the class is large, you may need a microphone so that everyone can hear. Eliminate ambient noise as much as possible. Arrange chairs and desks so that everyone can see who's speaking in formal situations if classroom arrangement permits. Of course, in class discussion it is generally more difficult for each speaker to be visible to others, and even more crucial is the fact that often a speaker cannot easily be heard by others. If this is the case, professors may need to repeat questions and comments so that all can follow the discussion. In explaining their difficulty in understanding class lectures, multilingual students commonly complain that professors speak with their backs to the class while writing on the whiteboard, thus taking away visual cues such as facial expressions and lip movement. This makes it harder for

them to hear and understand. If the professor or speaker faces the class when speaking, it is easier for all students to follow the lecture.

(2) Appeal to diverse learning styles and learning strategies by incorporating a variety of activities and presentation modes into classes. Learning styles can be categorized into three styles: visual, auditory and tactile-kinesthetic. (For more information about learning styles see Chapter 1.) Research suggests that native language as well as cultural background and experience may influence preferred learning styles and strategies. For example, if students have had little experience with group work, they may be uncomfortable with collaborative projects and with kinesthetic learning. Individuals tend to have preferences for a learning style, but no-one exclusively uses one mode. Using a variety of delivery methods for content allows students to explore different modes of learning and gives each a greater chance of being successful.

(3) Encourage students to take notes, even if the PowerPoint slides or other material are made available to them. The kinesthetic act of writing can help comprehension and reinforce learning. Taking notes requires making decisions about what is important and what isn't, what the main points are, what inferences are being made, and how the speaker feels about the topic/subject. Learning is increased when students must struggle with making these decisions. Students need not write in complete sentences or even use English. Encourage students not to simply copy from what is on the blackboard or the slides, but to add more.

(4) Use course management software where you can upload lecture Power-Point slides, assignments, deadlines and other class information. Today many faculty have course websites or use a course management system, such as Blackboard or I-Learn. With course information that is regularly updated on the course site, students can check information at any time (e.g. remind themselves of assignments, due dates and exam dates). Faculty can also easily send reminders and advice about assignments and upcoming events. Faculty can also upload links to articles, podcasts and supplemental readings. Additionally, faculty can upload podcasts of their lectures as well as any PowerPoint slides or other material used in lectures.

(5) Allow students to record your lectures if they wish to. If you do not upload your lectures as podcasts, students may ask if they can record your lectures. Having a recording of lectures gives students the opportunity to listen to the lectures again, check and add information to their notes, and gain a better understanding of the material.

(6) Help students in the audience become active listeners when classmates are presenting as well as when faculty lecture.

(a) Occasionally take a few minutes at the end of class and ask students to write down one thing they have learned in class that day or one or two questions they would like to ask. This can be done anonymously, thereby promoting more honest responses. Students can also be asked to respond to other types of questions (e.g. What is one area that you would like to know more about from today's lecture?). Collect the papers and read them to ascertain if students are grasping the material and/or have questions. This activity gives the students a moment to reflect on the day's lecture and/or discussion and provides faculty information about what students are absorbing. Allowing students to respond anonymously may reduce their anxiety and increase frankness. If anonymity is not an issue, students can be asked to share their observations with a small group in class or do an online posting.

(b) Have peers evaluate class presentations. For example, have a simple evaluation sheet for each presentation that a student in the audience completes anonymously. If there are three students giving a presentation one day, write the name of each presenter on an evaluation form and have three students in the audience complete the form anonymously and return the form to you. When you return your evaluation and comments to each presenter, you can include the peer evaluation also. (See the appendix for sample forms.)

(c) Assign specific students to ask at least one question of the presenter or group. For example, give a student in the audience a presenter's name and have her ask at least one question after the student's presentation.

(d) Inform students that they are responsible for the content of their classmates' presentations and include questions about the content of student presentations on discussion boards, blogs and/or on exams. You can even have each presenter submit a question about her speech for you to consider putting on exams. The object is to get the audience involved and actively listening to the presentations.

(7) Take a few minutes near the beginning of the semester to remind students of strategies for being an active listener and for getting the most out of any class. Possible strategies may include:

(a) Read the chapter before it is covered in class so that you are familiar with the content and the vocabulary. You need not understand everything, but the more familiar you are with the material, the easier it will be to comprehend the lecture.

(b) Take notes during class. You can take notes in whatever form works for you. The notes are for you and nobody else.

(c) Review any lecture material (e.g. slides, podcasts) as well as the chapter after the class. Rewrite your notes, adding information from the chapter and additional material, so that your notes are more complete. Make a notation next to items that you think are most important. Base your decisions about what is important on the lectures and discussions in class as well as the assigned readings on the subject.

(d) Write out any questions that you have about the material. Try to find the answer in your book, online or from a classmate. If you can't find the answer, then ask the professor before or after class or during her office hours. If your questions seem appropriate and are relevant to the material being covered in the next class, ask your question in class if you are comfortable doing so.

(e) Keep up with your readings and assignments. Try not to fall behind and don't leave reading the chapters until right before a test or wait until the night before an assignment is due to begin it. Plan ahead.

Understanding and Following Oral Directions

Like comprehending presentations, understanding and following directions is more complicated than it seems. Linguistic knowledge, decoding the language, pragmatics and background information (both content and formal background information) are required. Assignments, especially major ones, are generally written as well as discussed orally, so students have multiple opportunities to understand the assignment. Directions for in-class or informal assignments may be given only orally. For example, an instructor in an environmental science course may casually ask students to find a current article from a news source on a topic being covered in class (e.g. efforts in urban areas to increase 'green spaces' such as vertical gardens, roof gardens, community gardens, parks, open space) and bring it the next class period. Types of assignments that students are familiar with from their previous classroom experiences are, naturally, easier to understand and complete appropriately. Students familiar with writing up chemistry lab reports will not have to ask themselves 'What do I do first? What do I have to do?' Of course, with spoken directions difficulties with rate of speech and accents may arise. Multilingual students, as in formal situations and daily conversations, tend to have more difficulty with unfamiliar accents and the rate of speech than students who have more experience and facility with spoken English.

Practical tips to help students understand and follow directions

(1) Structure assignments and instructions carefully and be as clear as possible when giving instructions, thereby allowing students more opportunities for success and you, the faculty, more opportunities for receiving work that meets the requirements and your expectations. With class activities, directions are typically oral. 'Find a partner and discuss the progress you are making on your research paper.' These directions provide students much latitude, but faculty may wish to provide more direction for the discussion by giving specific questions that students must answer (e.g. What is your broad topic? What are two sources you have found, and why do you think they will be helpful to you? What challenges are you facing with this assignment? Offer advice to your partner.). Directions for assignments, especially major ones, are generally written as well as announced orally so students can read and refer to the instructions throughout the process. Instructions may be on a course website or distributed to students. However, typically there is oral discussion about the detailed instructions, with students being given the opportunity to ask questions and make comments. In order to assist students in completing the assignments appropriately, faculty can pay careful attention to word choice (e.g. *analyze, discuss, compare, contrast, define* all have different meanings) and understand what they are actually asking students to do by breaking down the assignment and/or instructions into individual required steps. For example, what must a student know to successfully answer the following question? 'How has the NAFTA agreement affected the lives of rural Mexicans?' To answer this question, students must know the main points of the NAFTA agreement, the daily lives of rural Mexicans before NAFTA, and the daily lives of rural Mexicans after NAFTA. Then they must be able to synthesize all this information, comparing and contrasting rural Mexicans' daily lives before and after NAFTA and determining which changes are the result of NAFTA and which are not. A seemingly straightforward question is, in fact, complicated, involving several steps.

(2) Be receptive to students asking questions for clarification about assignments, yet at the same time hold them responsible for following the directions.

(3) Offer suggestions to students for understanding assignments and completing them successfully. Here are a few suggestions for students:

    (a) Keep a planner or calendar on your phone, online or in hard copy, in which you write down assignments, appointments and other important commitments. Look at your calendar daily and manage your time according to your obligations.

(b) Look at each assignment carefully and make sure that you understand what is expected and when the assignment is due. Do this even if it is not due for several weeks. Ask any questions you have about the assignment.

(c) Attend a time management, study skills or other academic workshop that is offered on campus. If you are unaware of such workshops on campus, ask in the writing, speaking or learning center, and visit the counseling and psychological services to see what is available. The counseling and psychological services office on many campuses offers advice on dealing with such topics as deadlines, time management, schoolwork and stress.

(d) Get to know other students in each course so that you can discuss coursework and assignments. Consider forming a study group.

Multilingual students may ask for advice about ways to increase their listening comprehension in general. Here are suggestions, many of which multilingual students have told us:

(1) Listen to TED talks on the internet (http://www.ted.com/talks) on subjects that you find interesting. TED talks generally have subtitles and can be listened to repeatedly.

(2) Watch TV dramas, news and movies. If you have captioning in English available on TV, turn it on. DVDs often have English subtitles. Students have told us that movies and dramas also help them understand US culture and customs.

(3) Listen to news radio. They often repeat the same stories each hour, so you can hear the stories more than once.

(4) Talk with others in English whenever possible (e.g. roommates, classmates, friends, other students).

(5) Attend free lectures and events on campus.

(6) Use the tutors and teaching assistants (TAs) for classes as well as other campus resources such as the learning center, writing center and speaking center.

5 Reading

Reading does not consist merely of decoding the written word or language; rather it is preceded by and intertwined with knowledge of the world. Language and reality are dynamically interconnected. The understanding attained by critical reading of a text implies perceiving the relationship between text and context.
Paulo Freire and Donaldo Macedo (1987: 29)

The vocabulary is often difficult. It takes me a long time to look up words.
Graduate student from the People's Republic of China

Reading, perhaps more than the other three basic skills, seems to be a solitary activity, but, as Freire and Macedo (1987) point out, reading involves much more than simply deciphering the script of the language and then decoding the words and the sentences in a text. Good readers, like good listeners, are actively engaged with the text, doing such things as making predictions, asking questions, constantly checking and modifying predictions and rereading. They need to understand the relations within a sentence, among sentences, and among the various parts of the text. They need to unpack the text, that is, discover the deeper meaning of the text, including the author's implied meanings, cues and opinions. Readers' background knowledge, both content knowledge and formal knowledge (knowledge of organization and rhetorical styles of different types of texts), plays a crucial role in this unpacking of the text. In fact, Grellet (1981: 7) asserts that 'Reading is a constant process of guessing, and what one brings to the text is often more important than what one finds in it.' Research shows that 'when language *and* form *and* content are familiar and expected, reading is relatively easy but when one or the other or all are unfamiliar, efficiency, effectiveness, and success for the writer or the reader can be problematic' (Reid, 1993: 41). Grellet urges students when reading to 'use what they know to understand unknown elements, whether these are ideas or simple words' (Grellet, 1981: 7). He goes on to argue that using a global approach to reading, an approach focusing on overall meaning, is the best way to do that.

Researchers acknowledge different types of reading that individuals choose depending upon their purpose: (a) skimming – reading quickly to get the gist of a text; (b) scanning – reading quickly to find specific information such as a date, phone number or definition of a term; (c) extensive reading – reading longer passages, often for pleasure, globally in order to understand the overall meaning. Extensive reading develops fluency or comfort and overall ability in reading. Finally (d) intensive or close reading – reading shorter passages for specific information, often reading for detail. Intensive reading develops accuracy in reading, the ability to read and understand accurately the main ideas and details of a reading; in other words, to extract correct information from a text.

The purposes of different types of reading are not mutually exclusive. For example, we may first skim a book jacket to see if we wish to read the book and then read it from cover to cover. Another way to talk about reading is to categorize it as (a) for school or school-sponsored or (b) for pleasure or self-sponsored. There may be instances where a text is both school-sponsored or self-sponsored, but generally reading falls principally into only one category. The terms *school-sponsored* and *self-sponsored* are generally applied to writing tasks (Emig, 1971), yet they seem equally applicable to reading.

The link between reading and academic success seems intuitively obvious. Research (e.g. Carson, 1993) suggests that better writers tend to read more and be better readers than weaker writers. Additionally, research shows correlations between reading ability and syntactic complexity in writing (Carson, 1993). In his classic essay, 'Joining the literacy club,' Smith (1988: 2) argues that 'Children learn to read and write effectively only if they are admitted into a community of written languages users ... the "literacy club".' Using the metaphor of a club, Smith further argues that by being a member of the literacy club, one can gain membership in many other communities, including the academic one. Multilingual students may find themselves unprepared to be full members of the postsecondary literacy club and, indeed, may have never had full membership in any literacy club, even in their native or first language. They may do little self-sponsored reading, that is, reading for pleasure (e.g. magazines, newspapers, short stories, novels, nonfiction). They may struggle with reading, especially reading academic texts, and thereby experience challenges with other academic tasks, as many are built upon reading. Some multilingual students, especially Gen 1.5, may have low literacy skills in their heritage language, whereas others, typically international students, are well-educated, with excellent literacy skills in their native language. Literacy in one's native language means that skills, ideas and concepts can and do transfer to a second or third language. Therefore, individuals literate in their native language tend to acquire literacy in a second or third language faster than individuals who are illiterate in their first language (e.g. Ferris, 2009; Reid, 2006). Individuals who have literacy skills in one language do not need to relearn the concepts or skills, but rather they only need to learn the different surface features of the new language. This concept of transferability or of linguistic interdependence is captured by Cummins's hypothesis of a Common Underlying Proficiency (CUP) that posits there is a common store of conceptual knowledge that transfers across languages. He argues that linguistic interdependence is 'multi-directional and recursive' (García, 2009: 69).

The connection between reading and writing is particularly important, because the two skills constitute literacy skills, the mark of an 'educated' person. As Leki and Carson (1997) note, academic writing is seldom accomplished in isolation as it is generally in response to a text or information from a text, either print or multimedia. Academic tasks typically involve gathering information from sources such as lectures, textbooks and multimedia presentations; analyzing and synthesizing collected information; and incorporating information into one's response, whether it is via a written or spoken product (e.g. formal speeches, essay exam questions, comments in a discussion, research papers). Therefore, reading efficiently is crucial and at the same time, like listening, hard to measure directly. We make assumptions about students' reading ability based on their spoken and written products. Indeed, these products do indicate when a student has not understood the readings or lectures.

Multilingual students face numerous challenges in reading print and multimedia texts. Students often comment on four interconnected difficulties with reading in college: (a) the difficulty of the material; (b) the heavy reading load; (c) their slow reading speed; and (d) their limited time. Students may find the material difficult because of their unfamiliarity with the subject matter, unfamiliarity with the organization and rhetorical style, and unfamiliarity with the vocabulary. Students have often commented to us on the difficulty of a reading that has been assigned in a class, saying, 'I can read it, but I don't understand'. Students are frequently unable to read globally, getting lost in the details and unfamiliar words, and therefore have difficulty summarizing texts, that is, seeing the big picture. Beyond the difficulty of the material is the reality that multilingual students tend to read more slowly than native English speakers, so it simply takes them longer. Because reading is a process of guessing and making meaning, students need to use all they know to make sense of a text, whether it is written or via multimedia. They may attempt to read everything the same way and with the same purpose – a close reading, intensive reading. For example, they may stop to look up new words, not reading for overall meaning or guessing the meaning of words from the context. They may not skim a chapter first, reading headings, looking at figures and other graphics, but rather try to read the printed text closely from beginning to end. Their

Table 5.1 Academic reading tasks and the language skills involved

Academic reading tasks	Reading and proofreading peers' and one's own work	Reading and following directions
Examples: comprehending print and multimedia texts such as textbooks, fiction, nonfiction, academic journals, newspapers, websites, blogs and wikis	*Examples:* comprehending essays, reports, proposals, fiction, research papers and responses	*Examples:* understanding instructions for assignments, directions on quizzes and exams and procedures for completing reports and assignments
Listening – *Typically little listening is required, except with multimedia and audio presentations.* **Reading** – *Skills needed may vary according to the reading purpose.* (a) decoding words and phrases; (b) understanding the words and sentences in context; (c) understanding the organization and rhetorical style; (d) relating multimedia components to written texts; (e) relating the text to one's background knowledge and making meaning; (e) determining the relationships of ideas; (f) understanding authors' attitudes and stances. **Speaking** – *Typically no speaking is required, but there may be follow-up speaking activities.* **Writing** – (a) underlining or highlighting important parts; (b) annotating written texts; (c) making an outline or notes; (d) writing summaries and/or critiques. *(Students may perceive some of these as nonessential and do few of them. Some may be required at times.)*	**Listening** – *When reading others' work, students may be asked to discuss their reactions with the authors.* **Reading** – *Skills required are the same as those in reading other texts plus additional close reading skills. Again, the purpose of reading plays into the specific skills needed.* (a) deciphering others' handwriting if hand-written texts; (b) critically reading for content, organization and language usage; (c) close proofreading to comment on or improve grammar, word choice and mechanics. **Speaking** – *If discussion after peer editing is included,* (a) asking questions and giving comments on a written text to the author; (b) providing and receiving constructive and respectful comments. **Writing** – (a) completing a distributed peer evaluation sheet; (b) providing written response, questions and/or comments on the text.	**Listening** – understanding accompanying comments, questions and answers about directions and assignments. **Reading** – *Skills required are the same as those in reading other texts plus additional close reading skills.* (a) careful decoding of words and phrases (e.g. discuss, compare, analyze); (b) close reading to understand specific information (e.g. formatting, due dates, number of questions to answer); (c) relating the text and assignment/activity to content background knowledge and knowledge of the type of assignment. **Speaking** – asking questions or making comments about the directions. **Writing** – taking notes as needed to understand and complete the assignment.

habits can be counterproductive because the heavy reading load does not allow them the time to do such close reading for all the assigned material and often close reading isn't effective for their purpose. Students may not only have limited time because of their heavy study load but also because of their busy schedules. Students may work many hours a week, take a full course load, and have family obligations. Students may often feel stressed, get inadequate sleep, and, thus, not perform to the best of their abilities. Johns (1991), in interviews with politics faculty, found that students often have no plan when they begin reading and, thus, tend to employ ineffective reading strategies overall, stopping to look up unimportant words and failing to grasp the main ideas.

As Table 5.1 shows, the same basic reading skills are required in most situations: academic or school-sponsored reading, reading peers' and one's own writing, and reading directions. The readers' purpose and the type of text are important factors in determining what strategies readers should use in a particular situation. Good readers know this and use different reading strategies, depending upon their purpose and the text. For example, reading and following directions requires close reading, not simply reading to get the overall meaning of a text. On the other hand, reading a mystery for pleasure requires reading for global meaning, not close reading.

Not included in Table 5.1 is self-sponsored reading, but this is an important type of reading and one that overlaps with school-sponsored (academic) reading as well as the other two categories that we list: reading one's own and peers' texts, and reading directions. Like school-sponsored reading, self-sponsored reading requires different strategies, depending upon the readers' purpose and the text (e.g. close reading, reading for overall meaning).

Academic (School-Sponsored) Reading Tasks

When we think of reading for university courses, we think of academic texts and assigned readings: textbooks, academic articles, fiction, nonfiction and online material. Reading of more popular or less academic material (e.g. newspapers, magazines, blogs, websites) is often also required in classes today. For example, in an economics course students may be required to read *The Wall Street Journal* regularly as well as a textbook, articles in academic journals and websites. The type of text and the purpose for reading the text dictate strategies students should use when reading. Although multilingual students, and monolingual English speaking students, comment on the difficulty they encounter keeping up with required reading in their classes, faculty need not alter the amount or types of reading assigned. Faculty can, however, help students become more efficient and strategic readers. Below are some practical tips to help students with academic reading tasks as well as with reading in general.

Practical tips to help students with academic reading tasks

(1) Remind students that good readers read differently depending upon their purpose and the text. If one wishes to locate specific information, he scans the text, not reading carefully. On the other hand, one needs to do close reading and critical reading to get all the information from a text as well as the author's opinions and attitudes toward the subject. When assigning a text, if appropriate, inform students of strategies that will be successful in reading the assigned text, for example, read to get an overview of the structure of the US government, read so you can explain the differences in Jefferson's and Hamilton's opinions about the role of the federal government.

(2) Consider suggesting reading strategies to the class as a whole and especially to students who seek help or seem to be having difficulty with the readings. Below are strategies faculty can suggest:

(a) Encourage students to always skim or do pre-reading activities. Look at the headings, any graphics and any words that are in bold or are glossed to get an idea of the content and the organization of the reading. This strategy is especially useful with textbooks.

(b) Encourage students to keep reading and not to stop to look up each unfamiliar word. Students should try to guess the meaning from the context. If a word seems to be important, then look it up after reading the material completely once. If a word seems to be crucial for understanding, then look it up.

(c) Encourage students to highlight important items, make notes in their books and other readings, or make outlines of readings. A strategy that we find particularly helpful is the SQ3R method. The SQ3R method, developed in the 1940s by Robinson (1970), includes five steps: Survey, Question, Read, Recite and Review. This method, as the name suggests, asks students (1) to *Survey* or preview the reading, looking at headings, words in bold, graphics and so on; (2) to *Question*, working methodically through the text, turning the first heading (and subsequent ones) into a *Question*, thus arousing curiosity and improving comprehension; (3) to *Read* the text in order to answer the question; in other words, actively search for the answer to the question and take notes; (4) to *Recite* or recall the answer to the question, without looking at the text. Then repeat steps two through four for each heading until you have read the entire text; (5) to *Review*, after reading the entire passage in this way, *Review* and check your memory by reciting, mentally reviewing or writing the main points. It is important that students practice and take brief notes so that the SQ3R methods are accurate and efficient. Robinson (1970: 35) advises that the notes be 'exceedingly brief'. He goes on to caution against copying words from the text and taking detailed notes, asserting that 'many students copy a sentence into their notes without ever having read it for meaning' (Robinson, 1970: 35). The SQ3R method can help students be active readers and improve their comprehension.

A similar reading strategy is explained by Jacobus (2010: 1–2) who asserts that 'Critical reading usually involves the following processes: (a) prereading, (b) annotating, (c) questioning, (d) reviewing, and (e) forming your own ideas.'

We recommend giving students two cautions about these and similar reading strategies: (1) When taking notes, do not highlight everything or write extensive notes. (2) When writing notes, use your own words; don't simply copy words, phrases and sentences from the text. When reading, as when listening, students need to make decisions about what is most important, be able to put information into their own words, and be actively engaged in 'making meaning'.

(d) Encourage students to set time limits for their reading. A South American student told us of an effective method she uses. She uses a timer and makes herself read for 45 minutes and then takes a short break before resuming reading for another 45 minutes. After using this method for a semester, she said it helped her focus, made her a more efficient reader, and improved her comprehension.

(3) Provide assignments well ahead of time, whenever possible, so that students can allot sufficient time for the required reading. Often multilingual students read slowly and simply need more time to complete the readings. If the reading schedule is published online or in the syllabus, students can plan ahead. Of course, some students may wait until the last minute and find that they do not have sufficient time to do the assigned reading. Some, however, are conscientious and will use their time wisely.

(4) Encourage or require students to 'do something' with reading assignments. This can range from having students discuss specific readings online or in class to writing formal summaries and reactions. The goal

is to help students comprehend, process, work with and go beyond the readings. The type of follow-up assignment depends upon the type of reading, but here are a few possible tasks to help students read and comprehend assigned texts.

(a) Have students keep journals of assigned readings. Such journals can take various forms, one of which is the double-entry journal. With a double-entry journal, students divide each page, either paper or online, into two columns. On the left side, students write a summary of the section, article or chapter or write a quotation from the text. Then on the right side, they write down their response, questions, new vocabulary words or any comments they wish. Faculty need not grade the journals. They can tell students these journals will help them study for exams, get ideas for papers and discussions and so on, or if faculty wish to give points for doing the journals, they can read them a few times during the semester and give students credit for doing them.

(b) Provide students with questions to focus and guide their reading. These basically serve as study guides and as springboards for discussions. If students are asked to write their responses to these questions either online or on paper, faculty need not collect or grade these. These guides can also be used as study guides for exams, or study guides designed specifically for an exam can be distributed beforehand. The use of study guides for exams is controversial with some faculty arguing that students need to be able to decide what is important and that providing study guides or questions is spoon-feeding students. Others disagree. Whether or not to use study guides and how to use them are individual choices.

(c) Have students contribute to a discussion board, blog or wiki to summarize ideas, respond to provided questions or provide reflections on the readings. With large classes, students can be put into discussion groups. A different student, or group, can be asked to contribute questions for different readings to begin the discussion. Students can be required to read classmates' postings and respond to them. If time allows, faculty can read, respond and even grade each student's contribution. However, they need not do this. If there is a teaching assistant (TA), the TA can respond to each student's contribution or the postings as a whole. Students can be given credit for simply contributing, or the contributions can be evaluated, ranging from excellent to weak.

(d) Make students or small groups responsible for summarizing and leading discussions of supplemental readings, such as journal articles or other materials. For example, in an English literature class, one group could read and report on Edmund Spenser's epic poem *The Faerie Queene*, another on the romance *Sir Gawain and the Green Knight*, and another on one or two selections from Geoffrey Chaucer's *The Canterbury Tales*. Students can be held responsible for the information presented by each group but not required to read all three works. Either faculty can dictate the articles and additional materials for groups to report on, or groups can be required to find material on specific topics. If groups research and find articles to present to the whole class, faculty may wish to approve each group's selection of material.

(5) Inform students of resources available online and on campus, especially the library. Often time management workshops and tutors are available through a learning center or other academic support services office. Additionally, when telling students of resources, faculty can encourage students to find information themselves, in other words, to be independent learners. Often students simply ask the instructor a question, when the answer is easily available online or in the library. One way to help students be more autonomous learners is to simply refer students to places they can find answers, instead of giving them the answer. For example, a student wants to know the correct documentation format for a paper in psychology. Inform him that he needs to use APA (American Psychological Association) format and refer her to the library, a book, website or journal first. Offer to assist him if he has questions after checking out those sources. Often students simply don't know where to look for information.

(6) Encourage students to use campus resources to help them improve their reading skills. Many universities offer reading improvement courses and/or workshops through the learning center or college success programs. Find out what services your institution provides and inform students, especially those who express difficulty with the course readings.

(7) Encourage students to read more, both for school and for pleasure. Along with required texts, faculty can provide a suggested reading list; can inform students of related current articles and websites through class announcements, a course website or blog; and if students comment on their poor reading and vocabulary skills, faculty can answer that simply reading more for pleasure and for school can help improve their overall vocabulary and reading ability.

Reading Peers' and One's Own Work

To be successful in their classes and future careers, students need to become critical, close readers of their own and others' texts. Students are routinely asked to analyze an author's arguments (e.g. Niles Eldredge and Stephen Jay Gould's argument for punctuated equilibrium) and arguments for and against particular positions (e.g. a national identification card, universal health care coverage). An extension of these critical reading skills is reading their own and their peers' texts closely and, based on those readings, to revise and edit their own texts and offer suggestions to classmates for revisions, as well. As the second column in Table 5.1 outlines, when reading their own and classmates' written work, students must critically read for content, organization and general effectiveness of the text and do close reading, paying attention to smaller elements or local elements of the text (e.g. grammar, word choice, mechanics). Close reading is a different type of reading than is required for reading textbooks and some other academic assignments. Critical reading, regardless of the type of text, requires students to analyze the author's argument, rhetorical style and much more. These are difficult skills and developing them requires patience and practice. One way to help students develop these critical reading skills is to have them read and critique their peers' and their own texts.

Some faculty do not require students to read their classmates' texts because they feel it is not very beneficial and/or it takes up too much class time. In contrast other faculty may feel students learn much from reading and critiquing their classmates' papers and require students to comment on others' drafts online or in class. Regardless of what faculty decide to require, we suggest that they encourage students to read their peers' texts and have others read their papers for numerous reasons. First, in the real world, writers seek the critiques of peers on their written work and often collaborate with colleagues to write a text (e.g. a proposal, a bid for a contract, a professional article for submission to a journal or conference). Second, it is easier to read others' work critically than one's own writing. As writers, we often become attached to our words, we may not be able to view the text objectively, and we may be too close to the content as well as the written text. Third, students often are unaware of how they write in comparison to other students. This is often true for multilingual students who think others in the class write very well, whereas they don't. This judgment may be based on the fact that other students speak more in class and seem to have a better command of English or of the course material. We have had students tell us that after reading their peers' essays, they realize that their writing is 'not so bad' or that they understand that others have some of the same difficulties writing as they do. Fourth, students get ideas from reading other students' essays. When reading another person's text, students see what works and what doesn't work in a text and learn about the topic of the paper. Fifth, students may engage in conversations about the topics, content and essays themselves after reading others' work. Thus, they practice being part of a community of scholars. Sixth, students may feel that the ideas expressed in their writing and in follow-up conversations are valued by sharing and discussing them with others. Finally, by critically reading others' papers, students may develop skills that they can then apply to their own writing.

As important, or perhaps more important, than being able to read others' work is being able to critically read one's own work. Doing so allows one to revise and edit his writing so that it displays the content in the best way possible, with fewer weaknesses on the content, organizational and sentence level. Reading one's own work critically by definition is closely tied to writing, and we discuss the revising and editing process in the next chapter – Writing. Below is advice for helping students develop skills needed to critically read their peers' and their own writing.

Practical tips for reading peers' and one's own texts

(1) Encourage students to plan ahead so that they have time to proofread and edit their own work and, if possible, have others read their writing. Most campuses have a writing center and offer resources for students to work with tutors and/or faculty to improve their papers. Students may also ask roommates and/or friends to read over their papers and offer advice.

(2) Inform students of what type of help from others is admissible and appropriate. For instance, students should know that friends or tutors cannot rewrite their papers, correct all their grammatical errors or give them the content for papers. Faculty may wish to have some assignments in which students are explicitly told they must work alone and any assistance is not allowed.

(3) Provide students with strategies on how to give constructive criticism. Spack (2007: 276) asserts that in offering criticism to others that 'The trick is to place the criticism within a context of positive reinforcements . . . just simple diplomacy.' The goal of offering feedback is to help the writer, not to put the writer down.

(4) Encourage students to view comments on their work, whether from faculty or others, as an opportunity for improvement. Encourage students to be open to criticism and suggestions and to not become defensive. Encourage them to listen carefully and to consider suggestions offered in order to improve their papers. Of course, suggestions

from faculty on drafts carry more weight and should be taken more seriously than comments from writing tutors or others. In evaluating comments from non-faculty readers, students need to determine which criticism and suggestions seem valid and will improve their paper.

(5) If you ask students to peer edit others' papers online or on paper, provide guidelines and focused questions that reflect what is important for the assignment. (See the appendix for sample peer evaluation forms.)

(6) Have students complete self-reflection or evaluation forms on drafts of papers online or on paper. Students can bring these to conferences with you about their paper, submit them with their drafts, and use them to revise their drafts. (See the appendix for sample self-evaluation forms.)

Reading and Following Directions

It is often difficult for faculty to pinpoint the problem when students do not perform well or fail to follow directions. Does their poor performance mean they didn't understand the directions or the question? Does it mean they didn't know the answer or were unable or unwilling to follow the directions? In a math class, if a student submits exercises on page 13 and the assigned exercises were on page 30, this seems to be a careless mistake, yet is it? If the instructions were given orally, students may have misheard the page number as the numbers have similar pronunciations. But then, shouldn't a student be able to guess between the two page numbers based on what has been happening in class? Or couldn't he ask a classmate? To successfully understand written directions, individuals have to decode the actual words, do close reading and break down the instructions into the required steps. Many students have trouble doing this. In fact, colleagues complain that most students don't follow directions. Here is a typical example. On an exam, the instructions for a section read as follows: 'Identification: Identify or define 10 of the following terms and give an example of each.' With 15 terms listed, a student may define and give an example of only five terms. Does that mean he doesn't know the words *define* or *identify*? Does the student only know five of the terms? Another student may define 10 terms but fail to give an example of any of them. Again, does this mean the student doesn't know the lexical item 'example', has poor reading skills, doesn't read carefully or is inattentive, can't think of any examples or makes a conscious choice not to give examples? The answers to these questions aren't clear, yet in this example it is most likely the students didn't follow directions, didn't know the answers and/or had not read the directions carefully. Additionally, Johns (1991) notes that students often answer a question about an overarching issue addressed in a text with a list of details, some unrelated. For instance, this might be an essay exam question in a chemistry course: 'Explain the author's position on genetically engineered foods and the reasoning for his position.' This task requires students to analyze the author's arguments, to read between the lines, but first of all to understand the author's position on the issue. Clearly this requires close reading and critical analysis of the text. It may seem obvious what the author's position is, but students often have difficulty determining it. In responding to this question, students may resort to listing specifics from the text, some of which perhaps are minor or unrelated to the question.

Faculty cannot eliminate students' failure to follow directions. They can, however, take steps to minimize student misunderstandings, thus giving them the best chance to display their knowledge of the subject matter.

Practical tips to help students follow written directions

(1) Make the directions as clear as possible. Try to avoid ambiguity; use language precisely. One way to check for clarity is to mentally break down the directions into their multiple steps. For example, what does a student have to do to complete the task? Another way to check for clarity is to think about the end product, what you want from the student, and to work backwards to see what the student has to do to produce the desired results. For example, the essay question in a psychology course 'Compare and contrast schizophrenia and bipolar disorder and their possible treatments, with the advantages and disadvantages of each treatment' requires multiple steps: (a) knowing what schizophrenia and bipolar disorder are; (b) identifying the similarities and differences; (c) being able to list the possible treatments for each disorder and evaluating each; and (d) identifying the similarities and differences in treatments along with a critique of each. In addition to being able to do all this, students must organize the information into a coherent essay.

(2) Keep in mind that students may not be familiar with the type of assignment, so the instructions may be completely new. For example, if students are familiar with writing chemistry lab reports or business proposals, students will struggle less with the questions of 'What should I do?' or 'Where do I start?' Familiarity may, however, cause students small problems in that the format required might be slightly different from what they have done before. For this reason, we hear, sometimes with amazement, students say 'Professor X wanted us to do our lab reports ABC way. Your instructions seem different. Can I do it ABC way?' Even with slight variations in instructions, students who are

familiar with the overall type of assignment struggle less with following the instructions than those who find the type of assignment completely new. Providing clear and explicit instructions benefits all students.

(3) When appropriate, provide a model or template for written assignments. For example, in a science class, provide or refer students to a well-written lab report or a template. Such reference material helps students become familiar with genres in a specific discipline. In addition, consider providing an example on an exam, say a definition of a term and an example in an identification section of the test.

(4) Hold students accountable for understanding the directions. Of course, this means that faculty have the responsibility to write clear directions. Doing this is not necessarily a simple task. Students can be reminded to pay close attention to the directions; however, ultimately it is the students' responsibility to understand and follow directions. For example, if a student only answers five questions when the directions say answer 10, the student gets credit only for the ones he answered, despite his pleas that he didn't understand the directions. Likewise, a student who writes only a summary of a text when the directions are 'Analyze the author's argument on the use of genetically engineered foods' cannot receive full credit regardless of how accurate the summary is.

Multilingual students may ask for advice about ways to increase their vocabulary and reading skills in general. Here are suggestions, many of which multilingual students have told us they have found useful:

(1) Use an online or other dictionary to look up unfamiliar words.
(2) Develop your vocabulary through self-study. Use exercises in vocabulary books and online websites.
(3) Review new vocabulary words on a frequent and regular basis. A Korean undergraduate commented that she reviews new words whenever she can, even in the shower, often only for a short time.
(4) Read newspapers and magazines regularly. Read for pleasure as much as possible.
(5) Preview assigned readings, look up unfamiliar words and then review the readings.
(6) Use tutoring sessions, study groups and Teachings Assistants (TAs) to review readings and course material.
(7) Use campus resources such as the writing, learning and speaking centers.
(8) Enroll in reading improvement courses or workshops.

6 Writing

*Writing is difficult for me always, because it is not my first language.
I have a very hard time using effective vocabularies in my essay. Also grammar
is always a problem for me.*
Undergraduate US multilingual student

*I find it difficult to organize my thoughts when I write an essay because sometimes I do
not know what I should include or how I should organize my paper to be effective.*
Undergraduate international student

*For students to submit a paper is an act of being vulnerable. There are different ways
of looking at the students' work. With multilingual students, if there is a minor error only
every few lines, I think that's great. Other faculty may fail students for minor errors,
creating a paralyzing requirement for students.*
Rhetoric and Composition professor

Academic writing tasks are closely tied to reading, and less obviously to
listening and speaking. Academic writing is generally not done in isolation
but rather is frequently done in response to specific assignments that are
based on texts, written and oral, and on discussions. Just as in listening,
reading and speaking, student writers are active participants, engaging with
others. All language use is based on social interaction. The popular college
writing text *They Say, I Say*, by Graff and Birkenstein (2010), is based on the
premise that 'writing is a social, conversational act' where students must
summarize 'others ("they say") to set up one's own argument ("I say")'
(Graff & Birkenstein, 2010: xvi–xvii). They go on to assert that students
'can best develop their arguments not just by looking inward but by doing
what they often do in a good conversation with friends and family – by
listening carefully to what others are saying and engaging with other views'
(Graff & Birkenstein, 2010: xxvi). Not only do good writers engage in
conversations with others by summarizing and responding to others' ideas
in texts but also by considering their audience, the readers, and engaging in
conversation with them. Good writing is an act of entering conversations
with those who have written and spoken about the subject that one is
writing about and with one's imagined readers.

As Table 6.1 shows, writing tasks can be school-sponsored, either formal
or informal, or self-sponsored, categories proposed by Emig (1971). Although

writing tasks are diverse, many of the same skills are needed for each. Individuals often do not realize how frequently they actually write. This seems especially true of students today who text, blog, email, update social media pages and tweet as well as complete more traditional personal writing tasks such as making lists and doing creative writing. Self-sponsored writing may be in response to a text, either written or oral, but need not be and can be spontaneous (e.g. a tweet or text message) or carefully planned and carefully edited (e.g. poetry, a short story, a letter to the editor). Unlike self-sponsored writing, academic (school-sponsored) writing tends to be less spontaneous. We acknowledge that most writing that students do, even self-sponsored, can help them become better writers and realize that there are similarities in the various types of writing tasks. Here we focus on only two of these categories: formal academic (school-sponsored) writing tasks and informal academic (school-sponsored) writing tasks. We do, however, encourage faculty, whenever appropriate, to draw students' attention to how much they already write and encourage them to write for pleasure as well as for courses.

Formal Academic (School-Sponsored) Writing Tasks

Academic writing tends to be less spontaneous than writing for pleasure, and formal academic writing, when done well, is less spontaneous than informal writing. In formal academic writing, the process is recursive, not linear. Good writers do not produce a written text by going through a series of stages in a set order, but rather go back and forth among the steps. For example, while writing one revises, 're' plans, writes some more, incorporates and documents others' ideas, thinks about her audience and revises. Emig (1971: 39) defines prewriting as extending from when the writer begins thinking about the writing task to the time when she first puts words or phrases on paper/computer. Faculty's role in the planning stage affects the process in that if the directions are specific (e.g. topic, length, audience), students have fewer decisions they must make. Emig argues that 'a delicate balance, if not a paradox, exists in the giving of assignments' (Emig, 1971: 39). Giving too many specifics for a writing assignment makes some students feel restricted, yet giving too few makes other students feel at a loss about what to do. For example, some students thrive on the freedom to choose a specific topic that fits within a broad issue covered in the class while others want faculty to simply give them a specific topic. The type of writing assignment also influences how much direction faculty give students. It seems wise to assign a combination of very specific topics and self-selected topics from a broad range over a semester. This, indeed, is what

Table 6.1 Academic writing tasks and the language skills involved

Formal academic (school-sponsored) tasks	Informal academic (school-sponsored) tasks	Self-sponsored tasks (for personal use)
Examples: exam questions, essays, research papers, reports, analysis, proposals, summaries, case studies, webpages, creative writing	*Examples:* emails, notes, evaluations, postings, blogs, wikis, journals	*Examples:* diaries, emails, texts, blogs, entries on social media sites, creative writing, lists
Listening – understanding oral directions, questions and comments about assignments. **Reading** – (a) comprehending the directions; (b) understanding various texts, analyzing them, synthesizing the information and connecting it to one's individual content and formal background information to make meaning of the texts. **Speaking** – asking questions and making comments about assignments, the readings and one's written texts. **Writing** – *This is a recursive process, not linear, that begins after the prewriting stage.* (a) prewriting; (b) planning, including audience awareness; (c) actual composing/writing; (d) synthesizing and integrating information from numerous sources with one's ideas; (e) incorporating and documenting sources accurately; (f) revising and rewriting; (g) proofreading and editing.	**Listening** – understanding oral directions, questions and comments about assignments. **Reading** – (a) comprehending the directions; (b) understanding various texts, analyzing them, synthesizing the information and connecting it to one's individual content and formal background information. **Speaking** – asking questions and making comments about assignments, the readings and/or one's written work. **Writing** – *This is generally a less careful and less recursive process than formal writing, often with little or no planning or revising.*	**Listening** – *Students may write in response to something they heard, a film or other audio input.* **Reading** – *Students may write in response to a written text such as an email, tweet, blog, social media entry or print text.* **Speaking** – *Students may discuss their writings with others.* **Writing** – *These tasks range from spontaneous to careful planning, composing, revising and proofreading and editing.*

generally happens because of the nature of the assignments: There tends to be more flexibility in assignments such as research papers, group presentations and formal speeches than in other assignments such as summaries and responses to texts, lab reports and case studies.

As with the three other language skills (i.e. speaking, listening and reading), writing requires content and formal background knowledge, critical thinking skills, pragmatic knowledge and linguistic knowledge. Multilingual students may face challenges on all these levels. For example, students may be taking a required Western philosophy course and (a) may have little familiarity with any type of philosophy, either Eastern or Western (they have no content background knowledge with which to relate this new course information); (b) may be unfamiliar with the language and concepts presented (their lexicons do not have many of the terms used, and the sentence constructions may be very different from what they are used to); and/or (c) have never read or heard any texts in the genre of philosophy (they have little formal background knowledge about the typical organizational and rhetorical patterns used in philosophy texts, whether written or oral). Simply put, the first challenges are to comprehend the material, whether in reading texts or listening to lectures and discussions, and to think critically about it. Students face an additional challenge when they have writing assignments. Students are confronted with questions such as 'What do I write about? What do I think about this material and topic? How do I come up with my own idea? What readings and other information from other sources do I include? How do I incorporate them into the text? How do I organize the text? How do I construct individual sentences, paragraphs, and the whole essay?' They may not articulate these questions, yet students often make comments such as 'I don't know what I think. I don't have any ideas. I can't figure out how to organize the paper. I don't know how to document sources. My grammar skills are poor'. An undergraduate US multilingual student expressed her frustrations with writing when she said, 'Many times I don't know where to start with my paper/ thesis. Once I get started, I don't know if my writing is going in the right direction.' Students don't always realize that writing well is difficult for all of us, even for professional writers.

In university courses, students' writing is used to assess their learning of content and critical thinking skills whether it is on exams, blogs, discussion boards or in formal essays. Additionally, in formal assignments faculty expect students to write linguistically clear and sophisticated papers with a clear thesis, good support, synthesis of material from sources with accurate documentation, a coherent, easy to follow organization, and a rhetorical style appropriate for their specific discipline. However, these qualities faculty expect are often the very ones that multilingual students have difficulty with. Students comment that they have difficulty with writing on a number of levels. First, they may have little experience with academic writing. For example, European college students often have oral exams so are unfamiliar with written exams, formal essays or research papers.

Second, even if they are familiar with writing at school, the rhetorical style of written texts in their languages may be very different from typical Western academic writing styles. The study of the rhetorical styles of different languages, termed *contrastive rhetoric* or more recently termed *intercultural rhetoric*, has progressed far since the seminal work of Kaplan in 1966 in which he described the rhetorical styles of various language groups graphically, with the English rhetorical style portrayed as a straight arrow, Asian (which Kaplan terms *Oriental*) as circular and Semitic as zigzagged. While Kaplan has been criticized for his graphic representations, other researchers (e.g. Connor, 1996; Connor & Kaplan, 1987; Panetta, 2001) contend that preferences for rhetorical patterns, both oral and written discourse, vary from culture to culture. Indeed, Kaplan (1987) himself argues that the important thing is not what graphic or verbal representation is given to different cultural and linguistic rhetorical patterns but rather that different preferences do exist.

Instead of examining overall rhetorical patterns of writing in different languages, Hinds (1987) looked at the notion of reader responsibility for understanding a text, arguing that languages can be classified based on that notion. Hinds contends that:

> English places the responsibility for comprehension of a text on the writer whereas Japanese places the responsibility on the reader. Therefore, awareness of and attention to audience would seem to be less important in writing Japanese than in writing English. (Hafernik, 1991: 23)

Third, students may be unfamiliar with the genre of the discipline. There are similarities in Western academic writing styles across disciplines, but there are also differences in rhetorical style, organization, grammatical structures and even word choice across disciplines. For example, writing up an experiment in physics is very different than writing a report on a psychology experiment.

Fourth, much Western academic writing is thesis driven and calls for the students to form and support arguments; however, synthesizing others' ideas about a topic and formulating one's own ideas are difficult and often in sharp contrast to what multilingual students are used to doing.

Multilingual students may be from educational and cultural backgrounds in which students excel by memorizing and citing authorities, cultures in which students are not expected to express personal opinions. For example, Flaitz (2003) notes that in Korea, Taiwan and China rote memorization is heavily relied on and students are not encouraged to voice their own opinions orally or in writing whereas in Saudi Arabia 'students are encouraged to voice their opinions as this is considered to be a sign of excellence in a student' (Flaitz, 2003: 132). In an essay about learning English composition, Shen (1998) explains how he had to develop an 'English identity' by accepting certain values inherent in Anglo-American society (e.g. individualism and the meaning of 'I' and 'Be yourself') and by learning a new rhetorical style of writing (i.e. using topic sentences instead of the Chinese traditional style of 'reaching a topic gradually and "systematically" instead of "abruptly"' [Shen, 1998: 128]). A graduate student from Japan echoed Shen's idea of having an 'English identity'. He told us of a small incident that he thought exemplified the cultural differences between his 'English identity' and his 'Japanese identity'. Walking with his US roommate in a new area of the city where they lived, he asked 'Where is this place?' This was a translation of a common Japanese expression, to which his roommate replied, 'We'd never say that in English. We'd say "Where are we?"' In English, the 'we' or 'I' is the focus not the 'place'. The student went on to explain how this shift in focus, in speaking and writing, exemplifies his two identities: his Japanese identity and his English identity.

Fifth, multilingual students may lack sufficient linguistic skills to write high-quality academic papers. They may have original ideas that are ineffectively presented, and thus communication and clarity are weak. Faculty cannot be expected to be English writing instructors, spending class time on teaching writing. There are, however, actions faculty in all disciplines can take to help students become competent writers in their disciplines. In other words, faculty can introduce students to writing in their discipline and guide them to writing like professionals (e.g. a physicist, chemist, historian, educator, economist). Gaining skills needed to write like a professional does not happen overnight. Indeed a long apprenticeship is needed.

Practical tips to help students with academic (school-sponsored) writing tasks

(1) Assign formal papers well in advance so students have sufficient time to work on the paper. Of course, the amount of time needed depends upon the assignment. Regular written assignments that tend to be informal such as journals, lab reports or blogs do not require as much

planning as essays and research papers. The reality is that some students do not plan ahead no matter how much lead time they are given, but others will do a better job if given more time to plan, write and rewrite.

(2) Consider how written assignments are constructed. What are students being asked to do? How can the assignment or essay exam question be designed so that faculty get the response they want? Hashimoto (1991: 53) argues that in designing assignments, we need to 'emphasize the thinking behind the assignment making' and that our goal is to have students think critically about a subject and readings, not to simply have students give us a 'right' answer. Hashimoto offers numerous suggestions for 'assignment making'. Here we list only a few considerations he lists as 'rules of thumb': (a) 'build in room for negotiation' (Hashimoto, 1991: 66) allowing students the ability to convince us of the worth of a particular topic or a particular approach that they feel strongly about (this, of course, does not apply to essay exam questions); (b) 'have good reasons for assigning longer papers' (Hashimoto, 1991: 66); and (c) ask students to do more than explicate. 'It's not enough for students to explain what they've "found out" ... In academia, they have to do something with what they've "found out"' (Hashimoto, 1991: 54–55).

Another way to think about Hashimoto's last piece of advice is to consider Bloom's (1956) taxonomy of cognitive learning, which has six major categories that move from the simplest behavior to the most complex: knowledge, comprehension, application, analysis, synthesis, evaluation. Following Hashimoto's advice, we would design assignments that do more than ask for students to display their knowledge (e.g. define, describe, identify, label, list, match) and comprehension (e.g. distinguish, explain, generalize, give an example, summarize, paraphrase). Rather, assignments would ask them to 'do something' more difficult: apply knowledge, analyze material, synthesize information, evaluate material or make an argument.

(3) For major papers, require various stages where faculty and/or classmates can provide helpful feedback. Stages where written work is commonly submitted include (a) a tentative topic for approval by the faculty; (b) written progress reports at various intervals; (c) a formal outline; (d) an annotated bibliography or literature review; and (e) a draft, complete with documentation. Faculty need not review written work for each of these stages carefully or even at all. However, we do recommend that faculty approve all topics early in the process. Students can share progress reports and other stages in peer groups

and/or faculty can quickly look over some and make brief comments. Having students discuss their ideas and/or share outlines and drafts can help both writers and peer reviewers.

(4) Encourage students to focus on global issues or Higher Order Concerns (HOCs) first when drafting their papers and then to turn to Middle Order Concerns (MOCs) and Lower Order Concerns (LOCs). In composition studies, a distinction is made among HOCs such as thesis or focus, purpose and audience, organization, clarity and unity; MOCs such as paragraph development, transitions, tone and word choice; and LOCs or local concerns such as sentence structure, punctuation and spelling (e.g. Purdue OWL, 2010; Sharber, 2009). Some educators fold MOCs into one of the other categories so that there are only HOCs, global issues and LOCs, local issues. Whether there are two or three categories, global issues take priority over other issues. Students need to attend to HOCs first. Too often students fail to address global issues and become mired in 'correcting' their sentences. This is a self-defeating practice. If a paper displays perfect grammar and mechanics but has no focus, clarity or organization, it is not an effective paper. Of course, writing is not a linear process where one can deal with HOCs, then move on to MOCs, and finally pay attention to LOCs. The writing process is recursive, yet students need to realize that global issues are the most important elements. Faculty can help students focus on HOCs in their feedback, verbal and written, on drafts and in conversations about a paper. If the HOCs are weak in a paper, there is no need to be concerned about the MOCs and the LOCs because there is little content.

(5) Provide rubrics or other guidelines for major assignments that indicate what is expected. (See samples in the appendix.) Rubrics or guidelines serve as a checklist, indicating the importance of each component, for example, content, documentation, original ideas.

(6) Provide models or sample essays for assignments. Models can be successful and less successful work of past students who have given you permission to use their papers, or you can develop your own models. For example, if students are asked to write an annotated bibliography, a sample in your discipline provides students with guidelines for content and formatting. If time allows, discussion and evaluation of the models and sample assignments, in class or online, can help students recognize weaknesses and strengths of texts.

(7) Respond to writing, keeping in mind the priority of global concerns, especially clarity and comprehensibility. Avoid being distracted from the ideas by local issues. Targeted feedback can help students improve their papers by focusing on these global issues first and then turning

to local issues. Certainly, if a student paper is riddled with LOCs, such as grammar and punctuation mistakes, faculty can and should, as time allows, comment on this fact. However, simply writing on a paper 'You have too many grammar errors' may not be helpful. Focus on errors that hinder understanding and limit comments on local concerns to those. For example, if a faculty member notices a recurring problem with commas or verb tenses and forms, she can point that out to a student and suggest that the student consult a writing handbook or online writing resource such as Purdue Online Writing Lab (OWL).

(8) Have students complete peer evaluations of classmates' written texts, especially major written assignments such as essays and websites. Faculty can have students complete peer evaluation forms in class, outside of class, online or on paper. For example, faculty can require students to do peer evaluations of drafts outside of class, and then writers can use their peer's comments to revise their texts. Doing peer evaluations benefits both the writers and the reviewers. In order to make this process successful, however, faculty need to provide specific questions for reviewers so that they focus on what faculty think are most important. (See the appendix for sample peer evaluation forms.)

(9) Have students complete a self-evaluation of drafts and/or final copies of papers. Ask questions about global as well as local issues. On drafts, questions might include 'What is one area of your draft that you would like me to help you with?' Answering such a question helps students look at their own papers critically and identify what they perceive as their weakness, and then faculty can focus on the area students have identified as weak. (See the appendix for sample peer evaluation forms.)

(10) Tailor comments and evaluation to the assignment. For example, on formal academic assignments, faculty may wish to focus on the content of drafts to help students rewrite and improve their final paper. At the same time, faculty can draw students' attention to local concerns that detract from the effectiveness of the paper. Of course, with any assignment, comprehensibility and clarity are the most important elements. The questions to ask are 'Does the student's writing communicate?' 'Is it clear what the student is trying to say?' 'Is the paper effective?' and 'Does the student fulfill the assignment?'

(11) Refer students to campus and online resources to help them with the research and writing process. Most universities have learning and writing centers where students can receive assistance with their papers. Caution students, however, that they should not have others

correct and rewrite their papers or write their ideas down for them. Some faculty require students to indicate on their papers if they received assistance from the writing center, friends or others while working on the paper and require them to indicate the type of help they received. In addition to individual help, students often find online writing resources helpful. Many universities have an online writing center for enrolled students whereas other online writing labs (e.g. Purdue OWL) are open to the public.

(12) Be open to a variety of rhetorical styles and creativity as long as students' written work fulfills the assignment and is comprehensible and clear. Multilingual students often are more familiar with non-Western rhetorical styles than with Western academic forms. Although they may gain facility with Western rhetorical forms, it is unlikely that they will completely abandon more familiar styles. Rather, they may blend them in unique ways. Canagarajah (2006: 603) urges us to view 'diverse literacy traditions' as a 'resource, not a problem'. (See Chapter 8 for a discussion on assessing diverse rhetorical styles.)

Informal Academic Writing Tasks

Good writers employ many of the same skills for informal academic writing tasks that they use to effectively complete formal academic writing tasks. However, the reader's expectations may differ slightly when reading a formal academic text and an informal one. For example, faculty generally expect major assignments to be better written than informal postings, in-class responses, journals or emails. However, even with informal texts faculty expect students' writing to be effective overall. For example, they expect the student's text to fulfill the assignment, have a clear focus, be well-organized and contain comprehensible and relatively grammatical sentences. Most of the practical tips for formal academic writing tasks apply to informal tasks. Below we provide a few additional tips that specifically apply to informal writing tasks.

Practical tips for informal academic writing tasks

(1) Provide students with a variety of writing assignments throughout the semester, making sure to include informal tasks such as responses or reflections in class or online, discussion postings, journals and notes. Taking notes in class, reviewing them and rewriting them provides students with practice in writing as well as in listening. Having students keep reading journals can help them understand the texts and practice

summarizing others' ideas. In these journals, they can also write their own questions and ideas about the material. These activities are especially useful for multilingual students because they provide them more practice with the content and with writing. Faculty need not grade these informal writing tasks or can read them occasionally for the content, awarding a few points for completing the tasks.

(2) When appropriate, provide students with rules of etiquette for informal tasks. For example, if you require students to do periodic online post-ings on a discussion board or blog, distribute netiquette guidelines that you wish students to follow. These suggestions might include statements about being respectful in disagreeing with a classmate, about using texting terms and abbreviations, and about referring to articles or material in the class. Multilingual students, as well as native English speaking students, may not be aware of what is and isn't considered polite in academic forums. Often students do not make a distinction between informal language and formal language, using inappropriate words in academic contexts.

(3) Point out to students when they write an inappropriate email, posting or other informal piece and suggest alternatives. Generally, students do not intend to be rude. They simply do not know what is appropriate and inappropriate and what impression their texts make on others. A classic example is an email in which the student has no salutation, uses no capital letters or punctuation marks, uses emotives, doesn't sign her name and asks if she missed anything important in class because she overslept and missed class. We have seen such emails from all types of students, monolingual English speakers and multilingual students. Multilingual students may, however, be less aware of Western etiquette as regards emails and informal writing than other students. We encour-age faculty to privately let the student know how such an email reflects poorly on her and make suggestions for how to write professional emails and other informal texts.

7 Working in Groups

In Italy we seldom had group work, but we commonly studied with friends. The problem I have had with group work here is that other group members are not committed to the class and don't do their share of the work.
Undergraduate student from Italy

In group work, I learn from partners and classmates and have more time to communicate and talk about other things. It is nice to communicate with native speakers and my pronunciation has gotten better just hearing good English.
Graduate student from the People's Republic of China

Group work is common in US institutions for many reasons. As well as preparing students for the world of work, group projects can engage students with the material, actively involving them in the learning process. Researchers have documented the advantages of having students do group work: students practice and learn the skills of cooperation, collaboration, negotiation, compromise, responsibility and appreciation of others. Additionally, students learn more of the subject content because they are actively involved with the material, may gain a sense of a shared purpose, and may gain new insights and perspectives by working with individuals with whom they may not otherwise associate.

Group projects require planning and careful thought. Even when the project assignments are carefully planned, group work can be tricky. Many variables are at play with group work, including personalities, expectations, distribution of the work, commitments to doing quality work and scheduling constraints. Multilingual students who have not been educated in the United States may have little or no experience with group work in educational settings. Common problematic situations can arise even if multilingual students have some familiarity with group work as practiced in non-US or non-university-level educational settings. One common complaint is that a group really doesn't become a cohesive team working on a common objective. Members simply divide up the work, each person does his part, and all email their separate sections to one person who puts it all together. Individuals never meet to discuss the project, to agree upon the overall content and organization of the project, or to rehearse if there is an oral presentation. An international student commented that when doing group work with classmates in Mexico, they spent time together and got to know each other and sometimes became friends. Her experience in her home country was very different from what she encountered in the US where her groups seldom, if ever, met. She commented that she never got to know the other students in her groups in the US and that even if a member of her group saw her outside of class, the classmate didn't recognize or greet her. A Chinese international student told of another common situation: one or more group members feel that the work was unevenly distributed. He expressed his belief that with group work he ended up with the least desirable task, the one that required the most work. Another common situation all students may find themselves in is when the other group members care less about doing a good job and when individuals are simply irresponsible. In such situations, an unfair share of the work falls on the conscientious members, who make sure that the project is done well. Thereby, all members benefit from conscientious students' hard work. In sum, the structuring of group assignments as well as their assessment are important considerations for faculty. By carefully planning group projects and their assessment, faculty can minimize difficulties and increase the likelihood of success for all students.

Consider multiple factors when setting up peer groups and assigning group projects. Being able to work well with others is crucial in today's world, with employees often working as part of a team. This is especially true in business, natural and physical sciences, computer science and the health professions. A nursing faculty member stated that she felt part of her job was training future nurses to speak up as they will have to give opinions about appropriate medical treatment, defend their recommendations, and even challenge doctors and other supervisors who may argue for a different approach. Additionally, the workforce in the United States is becoming more and more linguistically and culturally diverse, and globalization demands interaction among peoples from different ethnic groups and countries. Today's diverse and rapidly changing work world means that individuals are often on teams with individuals very different from themselves. For short in-class activities such as discussions and exercises, faculty can have students work with one or two students sitting near them, can ask students to work with someone they do not know who is sitting near them, or if the furniture is not fixed and there is room for students to move around, can randomly assign groups. Over the course of a semester, faculty can ideally have students work with many of their classmates on in-class short discussions and exercises.

For extended group projects that require more than one period and go over several weeks, faculty need to deal with logistical concerns such as (a) the composition of the group, how to determine who's in a group and how many individuals to have in a group; (b) how to structure the assignment; and (c) how to evaluate the assignment and each participant's contribution.

There's not one best way to set up groups or to assign individuals to groups as much depends upon the size of the class, the subject matter, the task and the students. To maximize inclusiveness and ensure as much as possible that individuals are not excluded, we suggest that students not be allowed to self-select. When students self-select, they tend to choose friends, teammates or others like them as regards ethnicity, gender, age and so on. This means that individuals who do not fit into a major group may have difficulty becoming part of a group. Also, this often means that the multilingual students self-select into the same groups and native English speakers self-select into groups. However, the dangers inherent in allowing groups to self-select can be minimized if individuals are asked their interest and then faculty match students into groups. Possible ways that groups can be formed include:

(a) randomly (e.g. students draw numbers, count off or are grouped based on the first letter of their last or first name);
(b) based on students' content interest. This method can be problematic and similar to letting students self-select;
(c) based on assignment by faculty (e.g. faculty might wish to balance groups based on gender, language, culture, experience with the subject matter or other factors). This method can maximize the heterogeneity of each group.

Groups of three to five seem to work best as larger groups become unwieldy. If more than one group assignment is scheduled for the semester, the question arises as to whether students should remain in the same group all semester or form new groups for each assignment. Rotating groups throughout the semester has many advantages, the strongest ones being that students experience working with a variety of people and that students do not become pigeonholed into a certain role. Each group is a fresh start for individuals. Staying in the same group all semester also has advantages, especially if the group is cohesive and works well together. With the same group over several projects, students develop a work pattern and get to know each other better.

How group assignments are structured impacts each group's success. In deciding whether to include group projects as an assignment two questions seem crucial for faculty: what do I want students to learn by doing this project, and is having students do this as a group better than having them do this individually? After deciding to assign group projects, faculty must determine how to structure them. Certainly there are many ways to do this, with much depending upon factors such as the subject matter, the specific class, the students involved and the time available. Here we offer a few general suggestions.   ·

Suggestions for Structuring and Incorporating Effective Group Work

(1) Approve all topics early on and do not allow students to switch topics without approval. Offering feedback early on in the process helps students get off to a good start, minimizes opportunities for plagiarism, and saves time for everyone, faculty and students alike, in the long run. Faculty can assign specific projects (e.g. give groups different case studies or data to work with), can give students a list of approved narrowed down topics, or can provide a list of broad subjects for students to choose from and to narrow down into a workable issue.

(2) Include multiple steps and check-in points along the way. Again, this allows faculty to offer guidance and feedback, helps students focus on important issues, and minimizes faculty being surprised by the end result. These steps might include some but probably not all of the following: (a) a proposal for the project with a timeline and tentative outline; (b) one or more progress reports to the class via discussion board, blog, wiki or in-class discussions; (c) a formal outline submitted to faculty; (d) an annotated bibliography submitted to faculty; (e) group conference with the faculty; (f) report with notes on meetings of the group; and (g) an oral presentation to another group or to the class as a whole.

(3) Provide a rubric and/or clear information about how the projects will be graded. (See the appendix for sample rubrics.) In Chapter 8, we discuss assessment in more detail. The point here is that students should know how their work, including group projects, is assessed and what, in general terms, the faculty member is looking for in an 'A' project. Certainly, part of doing a project well is figuring out what to do and how to do it, and part of the grade is based on creativity and uniqueness. Nonetheless, faculty can provide guidelines and suggestions and at the same time not stifle individuality and creativity.

8 Assessment

I have been working on this tangle [assessment] not just because it is interesting and important in itself but because assessment tends so much to drive and control <u>teaching</u>. Much of what we do in the classroom is determined by the assessment structures we work under.

Peter Elbow (1993: 187)

This chapter is dedicated to the topic that has precipitated more questions than any other concerning multilingual students. Confusion can be expected because assessment is a complex issue involving multiple processes and is much more than simply placing a grade on an assignment or on the transcript. Assessment involves student expectations as well as teacher expectations and often introduces emotional reactions into what should otherwise be a fairly straightforward process. Assessment also relies on context and often includes issues such as attendance, participation and effort. It is helpful, then, to think of assessment as a sum of various components, each of which plays an important role in encouraging students' success.

The first component is deciding how the final product (e.g. an essay or oral presentation) or a behavior (e.g. participation, effort) will be evaluated. This involves providing guidelines that tell students the important factors that will be considered in evaluation. For instance, providing rubrics or checklists for an essay or formal speech when the assignment is given can help students prepare and understand the evaluation process. If students are expected to participate in class discussions, how much does participation count in the final grade? Is the quality of remarks taken into consideration or only that a student participates? Some of this information, especially about how behaviors are evaluated, is provided in the syllabus for the course; other information, such as evaluation guidelines for specific assignments, is given when the product is assigned.

The second component is responding to students' work in progress. We recommend that some review process for all major assignments be provided for all students before the final product is due. This step is particularly helpful for multilingual students. It may take the form of reading the rough draft or multiple drafts, providing individual conferences between the instructor and student, arranging for peer reviewers either in class or outside of class, encouraging appointments with the writing or learning center, critiquing a rehearsal of a speech or group presentation, or having the student report on progress at key points (e.g. a topic proposal or bibliography). At this time, the instructor will have an opportunity to make sure that the student understands the assignment, is using suitable resources, and is making an appropriate effort toward completion of the project. Feedback at this point will help assure a more successful product and make the final evaluation process easier.

The third component is the final evaluation, putting a grade on the product. This process should follow the evaluation guidelines given to the students with the assignment. Constructing a rubric or checklist from the guidelines that indicates areas of strength and weakness is helpful not only in determining the grade, but also in explaining to the student why a particular grade was given. (See the appendix for sample checklists and rubrics.) Grading is, as faculty are aware, the process most likely to provoke emotional reactions from students. Having a checklist helps dissipate both tears and anger to some extent; a checklist provides an apparently objective appraisal of the project itself and not the student. As we noted in Chapter 1, however, some multilingual students are under a great deal of pressure – either self-imposed or imposed by parents or even, in some cases, their governments – to get good grades. For these students, even a checklist may not be convincing evidence of a substandard product. At some point we simply have to say to them that we are convinced of the fairness and accuracy of the grade and explain the university's appeal process. If the student does file an appeal, the instructor should be prepared to present the evidence supporting the grade and should not take the student's protest as a personal criticism.

The fourth component of assessment is another form of feedback – making suggestions about how to improve future work, either orally or in writing. This is often overlooked, but it is extremely important for multilingual students. They want to improve, but they need guidance in exactly what to do. We recently saw a paper on which the instructor had written 'This is a good paper. Work on your grammar, C-.' We suggest that such comments are not helpful. First, if it is a good paper, the student will wonder why she received a C- and may feel the grading was unfair. Second, 'Work on your grammar' is so vague as to be confusing. Should the student study subjects and verbs? Comma use? Pronoun antecedents? Sentence completion? Syntax? If there are grammar problems that interfere with the reading of the paper, indicate specifically what they are and suggest a resource for help, in this case perhaps the writing center, a handbook or an online resource.

Keeping in mind these four essential components of assessment when reviewing student work will make the job easier, but certainly questions will still arise. We present, therefore, some Frequently Asked Questions about assessment that we have encountered with our faculty colleagues.

A Baker's Dozen: Frequently Asked Questions

(1) How much assistance seems appropriate for multilingual students to have on outside-of-class writing from tutors, friends, the learning center or the writing center?

How much outside assistance on written work to allow is an individual faculty decision, with the type of assignment and the amount of help provided as major considerations. Writing centers and learning centers exist to help students with their coursework and help them be academically successful. Most tutors do not correct each grammar mistake, but rather point out recurring errors that interfere with communication and also focus on global issues such as thesis, support and organization. They make broad suggestions for revision, but do not tell students what to do. We suggest that faculty encourage students to visit the writing and/or learning centers and have peers read outside-of-class essays. Faculty may designate that on specific assignments students must not receive any outside help (e.g. take-home exams, specific essays). The key point is for faculty to inform students of any policies regarding outside help in general and on specific assignments if there is any change to the general policy.

The degree of assistance permissible is not an absolute. Where is the line when the written product becomes more the tutor's than the student's? What kind of help is okay? These are not easy questions to answer. Students are often baffled by the line between 'help' and 'plagiarism', as are their friends who are only trying to help them. For example, if a multilingual student has her roommate help edit her essay for a sociology class, is it okay for the roommate to correct her grammar, rewrite awkward sentences or suggest she reorganize her essay in a particular way? In order to know if and how much outside help students are getting, faculty can have students indicate on their papers if they have received assistance from the writing or learning center or friends.

(2) Should multilingual students be given extra time on exams?

When asked this question, we reply with another question: 'Do other students get extra time?' Students have told us of faculty who regularly give multilingual students extra time for exams. On the surface this seems like a simple question, as did the last one. However, it is controversial. We recommend that multilingual students not be given extra time unless all students have extra time. In fact, once the time for class is over, faculty of small classes may choose to allow students who want to continue working on the exam to finish it in their offices or in the classroom if it is free. But then any student is allowed to do this, not only multilingual students.

Faculty are often simply trying to help multilingual students learn the material and do well in their classes. They want all students to succeed; they mean well. However, sometimes their actions do just the opposite. One afternoon, an international student came to the ESL director's office and said she had been sent from Disability Services. During the conversation the sequence of events became clear. Her social science professor asked her if she wanted extra time on the upcoming midterm exam. She had not thought that this was an option before, but replied 'Yes, I would.' The professor then told her all she needed to do was go to Disability Services on campus to receive authorization from the staff there that she could have extra time on the exam. At Disability Services, she was questioned about her disability and informed them that she had none. She relayed the instructions from her professor. Disability Services staff explained that being a non-native speaker of English was not a disability. The staff referred her to the ESL program director.

(3) Should multilingual students be allowed to use dictionaries during exams?

We get this seemingly simple question surprisingly frequently. We know that some faculty allow students to use dictionaries during exams; others ask our opinion on the subject. Faculty often tell us, 'These non-native English speaking students are at a disadvantage because they don't know some of the vocabulary on the test. I'd like to level the playing field. I want to let them use dictionaries. What do you think?' We typically ask, 'What is the class? Do all students have the opportunity to use dictionaries?' Our simple answer is 'We do not recommend that students be allowed to use dictionaries during exams, unless there is a compelling reason for all students to have dictionaries.' We have several reasons for this answer. First, to know the content of a given course, students need to know the specific vocabulary. For example, in an introductory biology class, students should know common terms in the field such as *natural selection* and *protective camouflage*. Second, students use time looking up words that should be spent focusing on answering the questions. Using a dictionary simply slows them down and does not, in reality, help them do better. Third, students may use multilingual dictionaries, in which the translations often provide many definitions for a given word, fail to capture contextual nuances and meanings of each definition, and may cause students to choose the wrong meaning. Fourth, students generally have electronic dictionaries, which have other capabilities such as holding notes and serving as a phone and texting device. Allowing the use of technological gadgets during an exam increases the opportunities for cheating. Fifth, all students in the class should have to meet the same requirements and be held to the same standards. If one student can use a dictionary, then all students should have that opportunity. Of course, there may be exceptional cases where allowing students to use dictionaries is appropriate based on the type of course and specific context.

(4) Should multilingual students be allowed to rewrite papers for better grades?

The basic answer is if other students can rewrite papers for better grades, then multilingual students should have the same option. Multilingual students should be treated the same as all other students. Therefore, if an instructor's policy is that a student can rewrite a paper with a grade of 'C' or lower for a possibly higher grade, then all students should be able to do that. If there is no such policy and a multilingual student asks to rewrite a paper for a higher grade, then unless there are extenuating circumstances the answer would be 'no', unless the instructor wishes to extend the opportunity to rewrite the paper to all students. The bottom line is that the same policy should apply to all students. By reviewing and commenting on students' drafts this question tends to be less of an issue.

(5) How much should grammar and mechanics count in the assessment of essays, essay exam questions and other written work?

When reading students' written texts, faculty often first notice grammatical errors, which they frequently label as 'glaring' and 'distracting'. Indeed, faculty complain to us that multilingual students end their sentences with a preposition, use articles (i.e. *the*, *a*, *an*) incorrectly, or mix up their verb tenses. Faculty also complain that students don't know how to use commas and other punctuation marks. The first complaints are about grammatical or surface level errors whereas the latter are about mechanical or punctuation mistakes. In judging mistakes a guiding principle is 'Does the text communicate?' 'Can I understand what the student is trying to say?' In other words, faculty must be able to comprehend what is written, minimally on a global level. If the linguistic or sentence level errors interfere with understanding, then the text is very weak. The next question is 'Is the text effective?'

The degree of linguistic 'correctness' demanded varies depending on several factors, the most obvious two being (a) the nature of the task and (b) the discipline. The type of writing is crucial in determining the importance of grammatical and mechanical accuracy. For example, on a timed essay question, multilingual students, and perhaps even native English speakers, cannot be expected to write flawless English; however, the meaning must be clear and there must be evidence that the student has adequately addressed the prompt. Simply including a few key terms in the answer does not mean the student knows or has critically thought about the content. If faculty cannot tell what the student is trying to say, or if faculty can't determine if the response is weak because of grammatical mistakes or because the student doesn't understand and hasn't thought critically about the content, faculty must assume that the student does not know the required concepts and content. Therefore, faculty should give little or no credit for the answer. On the other hand, a 20-page research paper that has gone through multiple drafts with feedback at numerous steps should have fewer surface errors and very few, if any, should interfere with comprehension. In fact, certain written products demand careful proofreading and editing (e.g. resume, cover letter, letter to the editor, article for submission to a professional journal). Johns (1999) also notes that multilingual students may never attain flawless grammar in their writing nor should they be expected to. In other words, multilingual writers do not 'become native speakers and writers'. Yet, she says that multilingual writers should recognize 'what kinds of texts should be error-free' and should seek assistance in editing such texts (Johns, 1999: 170). Certainly, her advice to seek editing assistance when needed applies to all writers, native speakers as well as multilingual students. Multilingual students, like native speakers, continue to improve their language skills throughout their college careers and beyond.

Besides the assignment itself, another consideration is determining how much weight to give to linguistic accuracy in the discipline. For instance, does a student in computer science need as much control of grammar and mechanics as one studying advertising or religious studies? Graduate programs and some undergraduate fields recognize that different language proficiencies are needed for different fields of study and have different entrance requirements, with law, nursing and MBA programs typically having higher requirements than math, engineering or chemistry.

Suggestions for helping students develop effective control of grammar and mechanics

(1) View and help students view grammar not as a set of restrictive rules, of *dos* and *don'ts*, but, as Clark (2010) argues, conceive of grammar in a different, 'special way'. In his book *The Glamour of Grammar: A Guide to the Magic and Mystery of Practical English*, Clark explains this attitude towards grammar when he says:

> This book invites you to embrace grammar in a special way, not as a set of rules but as a box of tools, strategies that will assist you in making meaning as a reader, writer, or speaker .... This type of grammar enables us to practice the three behaviors that mark us as literate human beings: it helps us write with power, read with a critical eye, and talk about how meaning is made. (Clark, 2010: 2)

Here Clark, and we, define grammar in the broadest sense to include not only syntax but also 'pronunciation, spelling, punctuation, syntax, usage, lexicography, etymology, language history, diction, semantics, rhetoric, literature, and poetics' (Clark, 2010: 4).

(2) Inform students of how heavily grammar and mechanics (e.g. punctuation) will factor into the grade for each assignment. For example, faculty often do not take points off on an exam for linguistic errors as long as they do not interfere with comprehension. If it is not clear that the student knows the answer to the question because of surface level errors, the answer should be counted wrong or, depending upon the degree of comprehensibility, the student only given partial credit. How 'correct' should a discussion posting be, a blog entry, an anatomy lab report, a 500-word essay written at home? Also, the stage of the work needs to be taken into account. In responding to a first draft of an essay, faculty should comment on repeated grammatical and mechanical mistakes that impede comprehension, but probably not mark the paper down. On a final paper, a portion of the grade may be for language usage or effectiveness (i.e. grammatical accuracy and clarity).

(3) Indicate the linguistic and mechanical weaknesses of texts and refer students to handbooks, online references and campus resources (e.g. the writing center or learning center) so that they can address their linguistic and mechanical weaknesses and learn the rules of usage. Use feedback to help them improve their writing skills.

(4) Discuss and, if possible, develop departmental-wide guidelines about how much grammar and mechanics count in the final grade for specific types of assignments, especially for major papers. Even if no agreement can be reached, the discussion among faculty can be beneficial. Some

faculty have commented to us that they would like to see a university-wide policy on the role of grammar in grading, whereas other faculty see no need for such a policy. Students, also, are confused about how much grammar counts in their grade. Students often comment to us that one professor in a department lowers a paper a letter grade for linguistic errors whereas other faculty say to students, 'I don't look at grammar'. In fact, this is what we hear from faculty also, with some faculty saying, 'There is no deduction in marks as long as I can understand the text, and there is evidence the student knows the concepts and content.' Students need to realize that requirements differ according to faculty and courses; therefore, it is essential for faculty to alert students to the importance they place on grammar and mechanics in each assignment.

(6) How can faculty deal with what they perceive as content-weak written and spoken texts?

This question, like many of the others, applies to all students, not just multilingual students. It is also closely tied to the following question regarding non-traditional Western rhetorical styles in that content, organization, logic and rhetorical styles are interconnected and influenced by culture. Below are suggestions for helping students, so are preemptive or preventative. The goal is to have students produce content-rich texts. Faculty can take supportive actions throughout the semester, when giving the assignments, and during the process of students' completing the assignments.

Suggestions for helping students develop content-rich texts

(1) Provide or refer students to models of texts that are rich in content and display discipline-specific conventions. Use assigned readings, supplementary material and student models as examples. Call students' attention to the rich content and conventions of the discipline.

(2) Read/listen to students' texts for meaning and overall communication. Multilingual students' written and oral texts may at first glance seem weak in content or weak in what we view as relevant content. Land and Whitley (2006) urge us, however, to suspend judgment and read for meaning first before dismissing information as irrelevant or the organization as illogical. At first, let the text and its topic develop slowly. This suggestion seems applicable to spoken as well as written texts.

(3) Whenever possible, have a conversation with a student whose text seems light on content so that she can clarify her meaning and reasoning. Sometimes by hearing the student explain what she was trying to

do, faculty can see why certain content was included or omitted and better help the student make the text more effective. The caution here is for faculty not to assume that the student has clearly expressed her desired meaning; the connections and content that seem illogical or irrelevant may be just that. On numerous occasions, we have been puzzled by the content included in a text, but after having the student explain her reasoning and the connection among ideas in the text, we understood why it was included, what she was trying to do, and could then offer suggestions for revision.

(4) Provide feedback and suggestions for improving the overall content of a text. Take the opportunity to help students understand how to incorporate content into discipline-specific texts in general, not just a specific assignment. View each assignment as a vehicle for helping students become more proficient in producing content rich texts.

(5) Help students understand the discipline specific practices of assignments as regards content. For example, students know what a summary is, but summary writing differs across disciplines. Johns (1999: 164) suggests that a summary in history is very different from a summary in philosophy, with the former being a one sentence summary of the argument plus analysis or critique whereas in philosophy this is not what is demanded. Students need to understand that one template for summaries is not necessarily acceptable in all disciplines.

(6) Hold all students to the requirements of the assignment. Even after taking steps to help students improve their content, faculty may feel the content is still too light, with some being irrelevant to the thesis of the paper, and that overall the text does not fulfill the assignment well. If this is the case, then the student's final grade should reflect that. Multilingual students, as well as native English speaking students, should have content- rich texts in order to receive good grades for their work.

(7) How can faculty evaluate non-traditional Western rhetorical or organizational styles?

As discussed in Chapter 6, rhetorical styles vary across cultures and to an extent across disciplines. Traditional Western rhetorical style is direct, with a clear thesis and supporting details and results in 'linear' prose (Kaplan, 1966) and a 'deductive logical arrangement' (Land & Whitley, 2006: 325). Land and Whitley (2006: 325) argue 'There are many patterns of cohesion, other logics, other myths through which views of the world may be constructed.' Genres in various disciplines also differ. Today, in certain disciplines, rhetorical styles are less rigid. Personal narratives may be considered evidence in the humanities and social sciences but not in other fields such as natural sciences and law. Additionally, what is considered acceptable and 'good writing' changes over time, not quickly but gradually. This is perhaps most obvious in creative texts, such as literature (e.g. English Victorian literature as compared with modern novels in English). Even in science, rhetorical and linguistic features have changed over time (e.g. Darwin's style in comparison with Hawking's). Land and Whitley (2006) argue that our culture and our language are becoming more pluralistic and, therefore, are changing; it seems inevitable that our rhetorical styles will do the same.

Multilingual students may be unfamiliar with the Western rhetorical style in general, with writing essays in English, and/or with the genre and conventions of a particular discipline (e.g. physics, advertising, philosophy). Certainly, multilingual students as well as native English speaking students must have an understanding of and a facility with disciplinary conventions of their major. As faculty it is our responsibility to help them acquire both. At the same time, it seems unrealistic that multilingual students will produce texts that are indistinguishable from the texts of native speakers (Land & Whitley, 2006: 325). We need to hold students accountable for producing effective texts that fulfill the assignment and that comply with important practices in the discipline. However, as long as student texts meet the requirements of an assignment, we can allow students to bring their rhetorical traditions to the task.

Suggestions for helping students develop effective rhetorical styles

(1) Provide or refer students to models of texts with appropriate rhetorical styles and organization when making and responding to specific assignments. This can be done when the assignment is given, when responding to texts, and when evaluating texts. As time allows, point out important features in the text that exemplify conventions of the discipline. If possible, have students analyze these conventions, by answering a list of questions or drawing up a list of important features (e.g. the different sections of a paper and their order: introduction, literature review, methods, results, discussion, conclusion). Tell students which conventions are most important, highlighting those needed in their texts.

(2) Avoid what Land and Whitley (2006: 330) term 'rhetoric-level myopia', a rigid, oversimplified notion of how essays should be structured when responding to and grading texts. Read for meaning and communication, allowing the text to unfold gradually. They urge us to 'broaden our concept of what constitutes "good work"' (Land & Whitley, 2006: 331).

This does not mean that 'anything goes'; rather it means that we as graders need to be flexible and open to different rhetorics. We can help students learn the conventions and at the same time stretch the boundaries for their own purposes. Canagarajah (2006) argues:

> [As well as making] students sensitive to the dominant conventions in each rhetorical context, we must also teach them to critically engage with them. We should help students demystify the dominant conventions behind a specific genre and shape writing to achieve a favorable voice and representation for themselves. (Canagarajah, 2006: 603)

He goes on to say that in such an environment, 'we will treat the first language and culture as a resource, not a problem. We will try to accommodate diverse literacy traditions – not keep them divided and separate' (Canagarjah, 2006: 603).

(3) Provide helpful feedback throughout the stages of an assignment so that students can learn from experience and modify ineffective rhetorical styles and practices. If an essay has an unclear argument or one that goes nowhere even on the final draft, point this out to the student. This is where a rubric or checklist can be of assistance to both the student, who knows exactly how her essay will be graded and was graded, and to the instructor, who can simply indicate the strengths and weaknesses of a product (e.g. the thesis is weak) by checking a box on the rubric or checklist. (See the appendix for sample evaluation tools.)

(4) Respond to student performance from a position of understanding the student and her experiences. Whenever possible, become familiar with rhetorical traditions students bring with them (e.g. Land & Whitley, 2006). By doing this, we may better understand why students use particular organizational styles and then be better able to help them learn the disciplinary practices. As our communities and campuses become more multicultural and multilingual, we have more opportunities to learn about rhetorical styles in texts. Multilingual students, themselves, can often tell you about how organization, logic and other rhetorical features differ in English from their native language. If the opportunity presents itself, ask them what differences they have noticed. By doing this, you learn about different rhetorical styles, and the student consciously thinks and talks about the issues of organization and style. In other words, she uses metalanguage about texts and experiences with texts and makes her learning more conscious.

(5) Ask the overall question 'How effectively does the text fulfill the assignment?' in evaluating the final product and assigning a grade. A subset of that basic question is 'Does the text meet the criteria outlined for students?' For native English as well as multilingual students, the answer to that basic question plays a major role in determining their grades.

(8) How much weight should accent and pronunciation be given in grading oral presentations?

It is important to keep in mind the distinction between accent and pronunciation. *Accent* is a pattern of pronunciation, generally associated with region, ethnicity or social class (e.g. a Texas accent, a Russian accent), whereas *pronunciation* is how one articulates a particular word (e.g. dictionaries provide appropriate pronunciations of words). Derwing and Munro (2009: 476) assert that 'One of the most salient aspects of speech is accent – either dialectal differences attributable to region or class, or phonological variations resulting from L1 influence on the L2.' They go on to note that speaking with an L2 accent has 'strong social, psychological, and communicative consequences' (Derwing & Munro, 2009: 476). People make judgments about others based on their accents, even taking an individual more seriously based on her accent. Some accents may be seen as more prestigious, but others are viewed negatively. In fact, researchers have found that individuals may experience discrimination in reaction to their accented speech (e.g. Lippi-Green, 1997). Derwing and Munro (2005: 379) argue that 'The phenomenon that we call foreign accent is a complex aspect of language that affects speakers and listeners in both perception and production and, consequently, in social interaction.'

Pronunciation and accent are important components of 'delivery' in oral presentations. Other characteristics that fall in the broad category of delivery include volume, rate of speech, eye contact and posture. As with other assignments, faculty need to inform students of how speeches or other oral contributions are graded. For instance, what percentage is based on delivery and what on content? Rubrics or other instruments can provide students guidance as well as serve as a grading sheet for faculty. (See the appendix for sample evaluation tools.)

The basic question in measuring the effectiveness of a student's delivery of a speech, and specifically of pronunciation, is 'Does the speaker communicate effectively?' Mutual intelligibility is the primary concern. The question is not whether the multilingual speaker sounds like a native English speaker; rather, the question is 'Can the audience understand what the speaker is saying?' This seems like a simple question to answer, but like so many of these questions there is no absolute boundary between what is comprehensible and what is incomprehensible. Indeed, individuals, students and faculty have different perceptions of accents. An accent one person finds intelligible may be unintelligible to others. Also, we cannot ignore the social ramifications of accent. The reality is that certain accents are perceived as more prestigious than others.

Suggestions for helping students develop effective pronunciation

(1) Recognize the distinction between *accent* and *pronunciation* and help students understand this distinction. Accent is generally tied to one's identity. Errors in pronunciation are often made simply because one doesn't know the correct pronunciation.

(2) Encourage students to determine and use the correct pronunciation of key terms, frequent words and proper nouns for oral presentations. Students can do this by using online dictionaries or asking others who are more familiar with the words. Students should be encouraged to practice the pronunciation of difficult words.

(3) Judge and grade students' delivery on the degree of intelligibility and comprehensibility. Does the student communicate effectively? As with grammar and rhetorical style, multilingual students cannot be expected to have native-like accents, though, in reality, some do. Faculty should try to judge the accent and pronunciation of students solely on the degree of intelligibility and comprehensibility.

(4) Be cognizant of the fact that listeners bear responsibility for comprehension and communication as well as speakers. Remind students of this also and help them become active listeners. All of us encounter a variety of accented speech patterns and in today's world this will only increase as the population becomes more diverse.

(5) Provide overall feedback to students on their delivery as well as the content and organization of oral presentations. Suggest concrete things for students to do to improve future presentations and their overall delivery effectiveness. (See Chapter 3: Speaking for more specific suggestions.)

(9) What is an appropriate weight for accuracy and fluency in grading oral work?

Two important components of oral presentations are (a) accuracy (grammatical correctness) and (b) fluency (the ease and evident comfort with which someone speaks). Although multilingual students can be fluent in that they are easily understood and seemingly feel comfortable using English, individuals fluent in English do not necessarily always speak accurately. They may have minor grammatical errors and use words incorrectly, none of which interfere with communication. In short, they communicate well and their speech flows relatively smoothly. Typically, Gen 1.5 students are fluent, having gone to high school in the United States and having used English with friends and at school for many years. In fact, they may be articulate and function within their larger family as translators and the ones who know English, helping parents and other relatives with transactions that must be conducted in English (e.g. accompanying them on visits to the doctor, to parent-teacher conferences for younger siblings). On the other hand, international students tend to be less fluent than Gen 1.5 students, generally having had fewer opportunities to use oral English because they have not lived in an English-speaking community. However, international students may be more accurate in that they have a greater command of English grammar rules and have had years of formal English education. We recall a middle-aged businessman from Japan who spoke accurately, but haltingly and slowly. It seemed important to him to speak very carefully so that there were no grammatical errors. He was relatively accurate; however, he was not fluent. He never spoke easily or smoothly. His lack of fluency made his speech, whether informal or formal, less effective.

Balancing fluency and accuracy when evaluating oral performances is a complex judgment call. The basic questions are 'Does the student communicate effectively? Can the audience or other participants in a conversation understand?' In a way these questions are similar to the one about accent and pronunciation. Is the student intelligible and comprehensible? In another way, the questions are similar to the one about grammatical 'correctness' (i.e. accuracy) in written work. As with written texts, the question is 'Does the lack of "correct" grammar interfere with comprehension?' In other words, are there global grammatical inaccuracies that make the speaker hard to understand?

The weight given to accuracy and fluency depends upon the type of assignment, the situation and faculty's priorities. For example, in a formal presentation faculty may expect greater control of grammar (i.e. accuracy) because students will have had time to practice and prepare. Nonetheless, there must be a minimum level of fluency for the presentation to be effective. When participating in class discussions and conversations, unlike in formal presentations, fluency may be more important than accuracy with the caveat that a student must have enough control of the grammar (i.e. accuracy) so that she is comprehensible. Keep in mind also that few multilingual students, or any of us, will display 'perfect' grammar.

Complete accuracy is not the objective; rather, the objective is effective communication.

Moreover, as with accent and pronunciation, listeners' perceptions of what is comprehensible and what is incomprehensible because of the levels of accuracy and fluency vary. We may have no trouble understanding a multilingual student while others may find the student's speech unintelligible.

We have been discussing speaking as if separate components (e.g. accuracy, fluency, accent, pronunciation), which fall under the rubric of 'delivery', are discrete items. They are and they aren't. In reality, it can be difficult to break speaking into separate components because all the aspects interact to produce an overall impression. To answer the initial question, *'What is an appropriate weight to give accuracy and fluency in grading oral work?'* we advocate tipping the scales towards fluency, provided the inaccuracies in language usage do not hinder effective communication.

Suggestions for helping students develop accuracy and fluency

(1) Indicate to students how grades are determined: the role of accuracy and fluency as well as the weight of content and organization versus delivery. The emphasis generally varies for each assignment, with formal presentations placing more emphasis on accuracy than informal tasks. For example, participation grades may be based on the amount and quality of the content of what is said, with little or no weight for accuracy as long as the student is comprehensible.

(2) Identify specific areas of weakness and suggest ways for students to improve future presentations and their speaking in general. Suggestions for helping students improve their speaking are in Chapter 3.

(10) How much should appropriate documentation and formatting count in written work and oral presentations?

Documenting sources accurately is important in all disciplines and, unlike rhetorical styles, is not variable. The style of documentation depends upon the discipline, whereas the weight placed on accurate documentation varies among faculty, courses and disciplines. Documentation errors border on and often cross over into plagiarism. In cases where errors seem like plagiarism, faculty need to surmise the intentionality of the author in making the errors. Was it a simple oversight to forget to include quotation marks around a statement when the source was cited? Was a student attempting to deceive the instructor by copying whole paragraphs from a source and not even including the source in the list of references? In these examples, the intentionality or non-intentionality seems easier to judge than in many other cases. In the end, faculty must judge documentation errors in light of all the student's work in the class and the type and preponderance of errors in a given text.

Suggestions for helping students document sources accurately

(1) Be explicit about what is expected in the way of documentation for each assignment. For example, faculty may decide that reflection papers with a common source for all students do not need a reference list but only need to indicate the author, title and date within the text. On the other hand, a research paper with multiple sources requires in-text citations, footnotes or endnotes as well as a reference list. For speeches, students can be required to submit a bibliography as well as give the references in their presentation. To help students understand the documentation form, refer them to journals, references in the library or websites to use as models. This information can be included on syllabi, individual assignments and/or course websites.

(2) Place a specific weight or percentage of the grade on documentation. In an introductory media studies class, for a five-page essay with three sources, documentation may be worth 5% of the grade, but for a 20-page research paper with at least 10 sources, formatting and documentation in an upper division course may count for 8%–10%. In certain disciplines and classes where documentation is emphasized, faculty may wish to take off points for each major error in documentation, perhaps a fraction of a point for each major error, setting an upper limit of 10 points.

(3) Use rubrics, checklists or other types of guidelines for assignments and for grading. By doing this, students know how much documentation and formatting count for in the grade. Rubrics can be tailored to specific assignments.

(4) Have a department policy regarding documentation, the type used, the importance of accurate documentation and formatting, and the possible weight for different types of assignments and in different level courses (e.g. lower division or upper division). If a department-wide policy is developed, it can be included with each syllabus. Faculty may not agree upon a department policy regarding documentation, but knowing what colleagues demand of students can be beneficial. Also, students need to realize and be told that individual faculty members may have different requirements as regards documentation and formatting. Each faculty member needs to be clear about her requirements.

(11) How can faculty assess group projects and assignments?

Many professors assign group work regularly for a variety of reasons: it is common practice in the work world, and it builds skills of cooperation, negotiation, responsibility, appreciation of others and more. In Chapter 7, we discussed planning and executing group projects. Here the question is how faculty grade such work. In answering this question, faculty need to take into consideration the nature of the assignment as well as how much the project grade counts in the final course grade. The process is as important, if not more, than the final product, and each needs to be evaluated. Faculty, through check-ins throughout the process, can ascertain how well the process is working and guide students, helping them learn how to work well with others. As with all assignments, students need to know how they will be evaluated: how the value and the quantity of their contributions as well as the quality of the final paper and/or presentation are to be assessed. We have heard many creative ways that faculty assess group assignments and here we provide a few possibilities and suggestions.

Possibilities and suggestions for assessing group work

(1) Assign all members of the group the same grade. This can be done whether the project is a presentation, paper or both. The advantages of this method are the simplicity of grading and the possibility of an increased incentive for students to collaborate and work together closely, thereby learning skills needed in the world of work. Of course, the assumption is that everyone is a contributing member. One difficulty is measuring the worth and quantity of the contribution of each member. Has each member done her share of the work? For example, for a communication class, students in groups of three need to design, implement, write up and orally present primary research (e.g. a survey, observation, interviews). Of course, ideally much of the work is done together (e.g. coming up with ideas, designing the study, gathering the data, reviewing drafts of the paper). However, when it comes to analyzing the data, writing the paper, and preparing for the presentation, generally group members agree to do different tasks. One student may analyze the data and write the methods and results section; another may write the introduction and literature review; the other may write the discussion and conclusion. Ideally, together they revise and edit the paper and plan the oral presentation. Of course, one person has to be responsible for formatting and getting the paper into its final form, another prepares the multimedia presentation, and all three participate in giving the presentation. For such a group, most faculty

would say all were contributing, and it seems fair for them to all receive the same grade.

(2) Assign individual grades for each person's contribution, either as part of the grade for the entire project or as a separate grade for contribution to the group. Ideally, all members of a group are serious and responsible, contributing throughout the process. However, some individuals, in fact, do little or none of the work, unfairly placing all the responsibility on those who are conscientious. Should such a student receive the 'A' the others have earned? One way to guard against this situation is to ask students to evaluate their own and their peers' contributions. For example, when submitting the final paper each student can be asked to submit an evaluation, listing the contributions of each member as well as her own contributions. In addition, each student can be asked to weigh each person's contribution, including her own, on a scale of 1 to 10. A student in the communication course could rate her contribution as '8' and write: 'I helped with all aspects of the project, analyzed the data in SPSS, wrote the methods, results and discussion section, and prepared the slides with the data and results for the oral presentation.' Instead of a 1 to 10 scale, other faculty ask students to assign a grade of A+ to F, for each member's contribution as well as for themselves. Assigning a grade for each group member places pressure, some faculty contend 'undue' pressure, on students, with some devaluing their own contributions or inflating their own contributions. If faculty choose to use self and/or peer evaluations, these can be factored into an individual's final grade for the project or can be a separate grade in the course, factoring into the final course grade but not into the project grade (e.g. all students receive the same grade for the project, 'C+', and then individual grades for their participation and contribution to the work.) In our experience, students inform faculty when there are serious problems with one or more group members. For instance, if one member has only attended one of numerous meetings and has not done any of the work, fellow group members often tell the professor before the project is due. Faculty can also get a sense of how students are cooperating as well as how the work is going through check-ins during the process (e.g. meeting with each group individually, having students give updates during class, having groups submit updates on the course website or blog). Also, faculty tend to have an overall sense of each student, knowing if a student attends class regularly and does well on other assignments. If it is clear that a student has done little or none of the work, faculty can give an individual student a different grade from the overall group grade.

(3) Assign a group project where part of the work is done as a group and another part is done individually. This seems most appropriate for certain types of projects such as having students collect and share data but analyze and write a paper individually with each focusing on different aspects of the data. For example, business students could conduct interviews with CEOs, share the information gleaned from the interviews and each write a separate paper. In this case, faculty need to indicate what is to be done as a group and what is to be done individually along with how much similarity there can be among papers. Moreover, ideally faculty will evaluate the contribution each member has made to the group as well as the individual's personal work.

These are only a few options for evaluating and grading group projects. Much depends upon the type of project, the discipline, the course and the level of the students. The most important thing is for faculty to think about issues of assessment when planning the project and to know and tell students how the assessment will be done from the beginning.

(12) What can faculty do to promote intellectual honesty and decrease acts of cheating and plagiarism in students' written and oral work?

A distinction is generally made between cheating on an exam or homework assignment and plagiarism, failing to appropriately document sources either intentionally or unintentionally. What constitutes cheating on an exam or in-class work seems easy to determine (e.g. using crib notes, copying others' work, using technology to find exam answers in real time, having someone else take one's seat for an exam); however, it is not always easy to detect cheating as it is happening. This seems especially true given cheating possibilities presented by technology. Cheating on outside-of-class work is even more difficult to detect. High-tech cheating or cybercheating on homework, as well as cheating, in general, seems to be widespread and on the rise (e.g. McCabe et al., 2001; Young, 2010).

What constitutes plagiarism is ambiguous, and as Hafernik et al. (2002) note, there are degrees of plagiarism, ranging from buying a paper, cyberplagiarism, to failing to document a source correctly in an essay or presentation. In between these extremes are incidents such as fabricating data, copying a few phrases or sentences without citing the source, and forgetting to include a source in the references. Plagiarism is not limited to written work but also can be found in speeches and other oral presentations. In all cases of plagiarism, faculty must make a determination about intentionality? Was the error in documentation made out of ignorance; was it a misunderstanding or oversight; or was it an intentional act?

Cheating and plagiarism cut across all student groups, both native English speakers and multilingual students. Students cheat for many reasons (e.g. pressure to get good grades, desire to get ahead, unpreparedness, pressures from family and friends, limited time to devote to studies, lack of confidence and self-esteem, lack of personal integrity) (e.g. McCabe, 2001; McCabe *et al.*, 2001). There is also a cultural dimension to cheating. In some countries one's results on an examination can determine a student's career and future, putting students under tremendous pressure to succeed. Indeed, we have had multilingual students tell us that they have to do whatever is necessary to be successful, even if it means cheating.

Second, the idea of 'ownership' of words and ideas is a Western concept. In some cultures, copying others' words or ideas is a compliment and a high form of flattery. Pennycook (1996) argues that 'the way ownership and creativity are understood within European and US contexts needs to be seen as a very cultural and historical development', and therefore it follows that 'plagiarism cannot be cast as a simple black-and-white issue', but rather 'it needs to be understood in terms of complex relationships between text, memory, and learning' (Pennycook, 1996: 201).

Third, in some cultures, in addition to the concept that ideas and words are not owned by an individual, helping a friend is seen as important even if it means giving her answers or doing her work. Leki (1992) points out that in other cultures:

> Knowledge may be thought of more as communal, less as individual property. The moral obligation to share, to cooperate, to help a friend or relative makes far more pressing demands on some of these students than the obligation our culture may wish to impose of individual work and competition. In other words, what we call cheating is not particularly uncommon or shocking for some of these students. It simply does not carry the onus it does here. (Leki, 1992: 54)

Our purpose here is not to treat the subject of cheating and plagiarism in depth but to offer suggestions for decreasing both. Universities, and individuals within the academic community, can promote academic honesty and reduce opportunities for cheating and plagiarism. Below are suggestions for doing that.

Suggestions for encouraging academic honesty among students

(1)   Include the institution's policies on cheating and plagiarism as well as campus resources on syllabi and course websites. Most institutions have statements about academic honesty in student and faculty handbooks and online. Many have honor codes that incoming students sign. Draw students' attention to this information.

(2)   Encourage students to use campus and other resources. There may also be resources available for classroom and individual use. For example, the International Center for Academic Integrity, a consortium of 360 institutions from around the world, maintains a website with handouts and links to member institutions that have resources on academic integrity. Campus libraries commonly have useful physical or online materials as do writing centers, speaking centers, learning centers and teaching effectiveness centers.

Remind students of these resources and policies as needed throughout the course.

(3)   At the beginning of the course, inform students about what assistance is permissible and what is not. In other words, provide students with definitions of cheating and plagiarism, and inform them of the consequences of cheating and plagiarism in your class. The reality is that multilingual students may not have a clear understanding of what constitutes cheating and plagiarism. Therefore, faculty can increase all students' understanding by providing clear definitions and examples. Faculty have much freedom in defining what constitutes cheating and plagiarism in their classes. For instance, is it okay for groups of students to do the math problems together, to help each other when writing a computer program in JAVA or to consult the textbook or class notes when completing an online quiz or assignment? Certainly there is value in having students work together to solve problems and grapple with material, but perhaps some assignments should be done alone. The answers to the above questions are individual faculty decisions, with variation across disciplines as well as among faculty within a discipline. A calculus instructor may urge her students to check the answers to problems in the back of the book or online before submitting them, or a chemistry instructor may allow students to use one or two formula sheets during an in-class exam. Faculty may even give open book exams. Without clarification of what constitutes cheating or plagiarism in a particular context (i.e. a specific class), students must decide for themselves and often they conclude that anything that has not been explicitly prohibited is acceptable.

(4)   Have a class discussion on cheating and plagiarism as time allows and when relevant (e.g. first day of class, when assigning a speech or written work that requires the use of sources). Consider bringing in samples of correctly done and plagiarized summaries of familiar texts for students to discuss and analyze in groups, deciding which summaries are correctly done, which ones are weak and which are clearly plagiarized.

(5)   Model citing sources in lectures, handouts and online, documenting sources in the format appropriate for the discipline. For example, have a list of references at the end of a PowerPoint lecture where research studies are discussed. Also, include the source on individual slides. Tell students sources used in preparing the lecture.

(6)   Draw students' attention to citations and references in assigned articles and readings. This need not take long. For example, if an article about the changing demographics in the South includes a table from the 2010 US Census, point out that the source is given below the table. Then make a direct connection to their papers and how to document statistics and other data.

(7)   During exams, whenever possible, space students in order to make it more difficult for them to look at other students' papers. Even when this is possible, faculty need to be diligent about proctoring the exam. In large classes, two or more proctors are ideal.

(8)   If the exam has multiple choice or objective questions, have different forms of the test and alternate the forms so that students sitting next to each other do not have the same form. The exams can have the same questions; however, the questions are simply in a different order. Additionally, in courses such as math or statistics, two or more versions of exams can have the same type of problems with different values in the problems so the answers are different.

(9)   Prohibit the use of and visible presence of cell phones, iPads and other electronic devices, including dictionaries, during exams. If electronic devices are allowed, have a specific reason for permitting their use (e.g. a calculator for math, economics or statistics exams). Technology provides more ways for cheating, such as texting a friend for an answer or accessing crib notes during an exam. We recommend students not be allowed to use electronic devices during exams, with the exception of calculators when appropriate.

(10)   With speeches and written work, make the assignments specific enough that it is hard for students to plagiarize or cheat. For example, do not allow students to write/speak on just anything. Consider giving students a broad topic and letting them narrow it, or have

students write or speak on texts that have been read and discussed in class. For example, if students in a business class have read and discussed four case studies, assign students to choose one of them to use for their speech or written analysis. Other possible related actions include the following:

(a) Approve all topics and any changes.
(b) Have check-ins for longer work (e.g. list of sources, outline and thesis, progress reports).
(c) Have students submit copies of their sources with their speech or papers.
(d) Have them submit the speaking notes immediately after giving their speech.

(11) On written and oral assignments, have students sign a statement that the work they are submitting is their own. This can be for major assignments, exams and homework when faculty want students not to collaborate with others or receive outside help. Alternatively, faculty may wish to have students sign a contract at the beginning of the semester indicating that they understand and agree to the institution's and individual course policies, including the policy on cheating and plagiarism.

(12) Encourage discussion of academic honesty within and across departments as well as university wide. These discussions can be among faculty, staff, administrators and students, including student organizations. Various units and departments generally offer student workshops on academic honesty. These multiple efforts can help create a culture of academic integrity on campus, an environment where academic honesty is highly valued.

(13) How can faculty deal with acts of cheating and plagiarism in different types of assignments?

This question is closely tied to the last one in that it deals with cheating and plagiarism. The difference is that this question is about what faculty do when they discover that a student has cheated on an exam or homework or committed plagiarism, either in a written or oral assignment. Institutions may spell out explicit penalties for specific acts of cheating (e.g. using crib notes on an exam) or plagiarism (e.g. having another student write a paper), but most institutions have more general policies that provide a range of consequences (e.g. ranging from receiving an 'F' on a clearly plagiarized paper to being dismissed from the institution).

There is no one answer to this broad question as there are degrees of cheating the same as there are degrees of plagiarism. Is helping another student with her homework math problems, maybe even showing her how to do the problem, cheating? Is it cheating to copy an engineering problem from online, with each step of the problem clearly explained? These incidents are clearly different from blatant cheating on an exam by copying answers from another student or using an electronic or paper crib sheet.

As well as looking at the degree of the alleged act of cheating or plagiarism, faculty need to consider the motivation of the student: the intentionality or unintentionality. Students may not know how to correctly cite and document sources for a variety of reasons, including cultural factors. Bloch (2012: 145), in a blog discussion with students about plagiarism, found that students felt that 'intentionality was a critical factor in determining how instances of plagiarism should be dealt with'.

Suggestions for dealing with acts of cheating and plagiarism

(1) Be consistent in applying the institutional policies and rules within a class, taking into consideration the degree of the infraction and the objectives of the assignment as well as what students can reasonably be expected to understand of US academic honesty. Determining the intentionality of acts of cheating and plagiarism is often difficult and is largely based on the information you know that students have been given (e.g. policies regarding cheating and plagiarism, discussion in class on these topics). We have had students, multilingual and US monolingual English speakers, plead ignorance of good practices of academic honesty. Often these pleas are unconvincing. Provide students clear guidelines for what constitutes academic integrity, and then use the same policies for multilingual students as for native English speaking students. In a composition class where students are learning to write a research paper, faculty may not penalize students for small acts of plagiarism (e.g. documented sentences copied but without quotation marks, statistics provided without the source indicated) on a draft, but rather use such incidents to review and practice in-text citations. However, if these errors remain in the final draft, it's appropriate to mark the paper down one or two letter grades, depending on the types and number of infractions. In general, faculty may wish to give students a warning the first time small infractions occur and then hold them accountable with all future assignments. Serious violations seem to be a different matter all together.

(2) Gather evidence of suspected plagiarism and then provide the student with the opportunity to explain. Some faculty require students to submit all their papers through a plagiarism detection software program, whereas other faculty feel such software often leads to students being

falsely accused of plagiarism. Simply having students use the plagiarism detection software may act as a deterrent in that students fear being caught. In addition to such software, search engines can often detect plagiarized sentences. If a student admits to blatantly plagiarizing a paper or there is irrefutable evidence and it is the first offense, faculty may wish to allow the student to rewrite the paper within a specified period of time, with, for example, 'C' being the highest possible grade; may wish to give the student a '0' for the paper; or may devise another option. The hope is that the incident is turned into a learning experience for the student.

(3) Discuss how to handle cheating and plagiarism in department meetings and wider campus venues, giving special attention to cultural dimensions of plagiarism. Such discussions can lead to the development of a statement to be included on all course syllabi within a department, college or institution.

(4) Work to promote academic integrity and to create a culture that values academic integrity. Doing this is not a faculty issue only, nor is it a one-time effort. There needs to be a commitment to adhere to and enforce policies of academic integrity and to keep the topic in the forefront. Vigilance is required. Faculty and students soon learn if there is little support for and enforcement of institutional policies regarding academic dishonesty. If a faculty member gives a failing grade to a student who cheats or commits a blatant act of plagiarism and finds little support for her action, this faculty member will hesitate to 'hold the line' in future cases. The result is that students will soon learn that the policies are seldom enforced and that the consequences for violating the rules or honor code are small. Of course, institutions must guard students' rights, and this includes a student's right to appeal a grade. In short, the entire academic community must work together to promote academic integrity and reduce cheating and plagiarism and at the same time protect students' rights.

Epilogue: Outside the Ivory Tower

*What we are witnessing is a mad dash – born of fifty years of pent-up aspirations
in places like India, China, and the former Soviet Empire, where for five decades
young people were educated, but not given an outlet at home to really fulfill their potential.
Imagine shaking a champagne bottle for fifty years and then finally uncorking it.
You get quite a pop when the cork comes off. You don't want to get in the way of that cork.*
Thomas Friedman (2006: 214)

In this book we have focused almost solely on the classroom experience; it is now time to step outside our classrooms and take notice of the larger world.

For some 30 years now, globalization has been a political and economic reality in our world. Thomas Friedman (2006) gives us a stark look at this reality in *The World is Flat: A Brief History of the Twenty-First Century*, an examination of how science and technology have reshaped world trade and communication and how central education is to our ability to confront this reality.

Friedman makes it clear that globalization is now becoming an academic reality as well, as more and more students come to the United States for their education, and then return to their home countries with the language and ideas they have gained from our universities. At the same time, the faculty and staff at universities are more and more diverse in terms of ethnicity, culture, gender and lifestyle. This new academic reality is also becoming clear as more and more immigrant and US multilingual individuals impact and join 'mainstream' US culture.

The presence of an increasingly large immigrant and international population is not just a temporary bump; it is our future. The United States Department of Education projects that from 2011 to 2019 US college enrollment of Hispanics will increase by 36.8%, Nonresident Aliens (i.e. international students) by 24.5%, Black non-Hispanics by 24.4%, and Asian and Pacific Islanders by 23.4%. During the same interval White, non-Hispanic enrollment is expected to increase by only 5.2% (The Chronicle of Higher Education, 2011: 32).

Our attention on international students should not, however, blind us from seeing the potential that resident multilingual students bring to our classrooms. It is they who are perhaps best equipped to understand and function in an increasingly flattened world. They can be a bridge between our domestic students who have a US-centric worldview and our international contacts who see the world from the perspectives of their home countries.

In order to prepare all students for this new globalization, we need to encourage students to learn more about other cultures and peoples, to interact with students from other nations and cultures, and to become, and see themselves as, citizens of the world. We can do this by encouraging students to study abroad, to learn from multilingual students in their classes and on campuses, and to realize that students from other cultures and nations are valuable resources for us all.

Our world is changing, and we must change with it. There are two paths we in academia can take: (a) Ignore the reality and hope it will change; or (b) Seize upon it as an opportunity to produce the best-educated, most globally-aware citizens that we can. Clearly the second path is not only the most responsible, but the most desirable, and can result in better lives for all our students, regardless of their country or language of origin.

Our universities, our classrooms, our campuses are the places that this transformation of all our students – both domestic and international – into global citizens can best begin, and it is there we have the opportunity to impact the future. To do so we must, as we noted in nearly every chapter of this book, view our multilingual speakers not as problems, but as a resource; not as those with deficits, but as those with possibilities. Fully integrating multilingual students into our classrooms requires understanding and commitment based on the principles we outlined in the Introduction:

(1) Multilingualism is positive and should be encouraged.
(2) Emerging English proficiency and limited awareness of US academic norms do not mean limited intelligence or limited academic ability.
(3) Compartmentalizing courses or marginalizing multilingual students is counterproductive for all members of the academy.
(4) Labels such as 'remedial' or 'developmental' to describe multilingual speakers are seductive and misleading.
(5) All faculty can and should assist multilingual students in improving their English proficiency and their knowledge of 'how to be' a member of the academy.

We realize, of course, that although it is easy for us to advocate these positions, putting them into practice in the classroom may be much more difficult. We have provided some ideas that we and others have found to be successful in implementing a globally diverse classroom. We have analyzed some of the essential classroom tasks to illustrate the complexity of the barriers our multilingual students encounter, and we have addressed a variety of ways to make those tasks more productive and, yes, more pleasant.

We are also aware, however, that simply knowing a few tips to help our students is seldom enough. In order to move from the university to the world, we must vacate our comfort zones and try new ways of teaching and new views of curriculum. As we gain a new appreciation of culturally and ethnically diverse classrooms, we will take more responsibility for helping to socialize our students into the academy and the world.

Finally, our concept of the university itself is being changed by the emergence of multilingual students as an increasingly significant portion of our enrollment. The university of the future will not be like the university of the past, or even the present. It will evolve and change, in both obvious and subtle ways. Part of that change will be instigated by the presence of multilingual students. This is much bigger than just leaving our comfort zones – it is our challenge for the future of the academy.

References

Bartholomae, D. (2003) Inventing the university. In C. Glenn, M.A. Goldthwaite and R. Connors (eds) *The St. Martin's Guide to Teaching Writing* (5th edn, pp. 403–417). Boston: Bedford/St. Martin's. (Original work published 1985)

Barton, D. and Tusting, K. (eds) (2005) *Beyond Communities of Practice: Language, Power, and Social Context*. New York: Cambridge University Press.

Benesch, S. (2009) Interrogating in-between-ness: A post-modern perspective on immigrant students. In M. Roberge, M. Siegal and L. Harklau (eds) *Generation 1.5 in College Composition: Teaching Academic Writing to US Educated Learners of ESL* (pp. 65–72). New York: Routledge.

Berkenkotter, C. and Huckin, T. (1995) *Genre Knowledge in Disciplinary Communication: Cognition/Culture/Power*. Hillsdale, NJ: Lawrence Erlbaum.

Bizzell, P. (1982) College composition: Initiation into the academic discourse community. *Curriculum Inquiry* 12, 191–207.

Blanton, L.L. (1999) Classroom instruction and language minority students: On teaching to 'smarter' readers and writers. In L. Harklau, K.M. Losey and M. Siegal (eds) *Generation 1.5 Meets College Composition: Issues in the Teaching of Writing to US-Educated Learners of ESL* (pp. 119–142). Mahwah, NJ: Lawrence Erlbaum.

Bloch, J. (2012) *Plagiarism, Intellectual Property and the Teaching of L2 Writing*. Bristol: Multilingual Matters.

Bloom, B.S. (1956) *Taxonomy of Educational Objectives. Handbook I: The Cognitive Domain*. New York: David McKay Co., Inc.

Canagarajah, A.S. (1999) Interrogating the 'native speaker fallacy': Non-linguistic roots, non-pedagogical results. In G. Braine (ed.) *Non-Native Educators in English Language Teaching* (pp. 77–92). Mahwah, NJ: Lawrence Erlbaum.

Canagarajah, A.S. (2006) Understanding critical writing. In P.K. Matsuda, M. Cox, J. Jordan and C. Ortmeier-Hooper (eds) *Second-Language Writing in the Composition Classroom: A Critical Sourcebook* (pp. 210–224). Boston: Bedford/St. Martin's. (Original work published 2002)

Carr, N. (2008, July/August) Is Google making us stupid? What the internet is doing to our brains. *The Atlantic Magazine*. Online document: http://www.theatlantic.com/magazine/archive/2008/07/is-google-making-us-stupid/6868/. Accessed 15.07.12.

Carrell, P.L. (1983) Some issues in studying the role of schemata, or background knowledge, in second language comprehension. *Reading in a Foreign Language* 1(2), 81–92.

Carrell, P.L. (1990) Reading in a foreign language: Research and pedagogy. *JALT Journal* 12 (1), 53–74.

Carson, J.G. (1993) Reading for writing: Cognitive perspectives. In J.G. Carson and I. Leki (eds) *Reading in the Composition Classroom: Second Language Perspectives* (pp. 85–104). Boston, MA: Heinle and Heinle.

Chiang, Y.S.D. and Schmida, M. (1999) Language identity and language ownership: Linguistic conflicts of first-year university writing students. In L. Harklau, K.M. Losey and M. Siegal (eds) *Generation 1.5 Meets College Composition: Issues in the*

Teaching of Writing to US-Educated Learners of ESL (pp. 81–96). Mahwah, NJ: Lawrence Erlbaum.

The Chronicle of Higher Education, Almanac Issue: 2011–2012. (2011, August 26) Online at: http://chronicle.com/section/Almanac-of-Higher-Education/536/. Accessed 15.07.12.

Clark, R.P. (2010) *The Glamour of Grammar: A Guide to the Magic and Mystery of Practical English.* New York: Little, Brown and Company.

Collier, V. (1987) Age and rate of acquisition of second languages for academic purposes. *TESOL Quarterly* 21, 617–641.

Collier, V. (1989) How long? A synthesis of research on academic achievement in a second language. *TESOL Quarterly* 23, 509–513.

Connor, U. (1996) *Contrastive Rhetoric: Cross-Cultural Aspects of Second-Language Writing.* Cambridge, UK: Cambridge University Press.

Connor, U. and Kaplan, R.B. (eds) (1987) *Writing Across Languages: Analysis of L2 Text.* Reading, MA: Addison-Wesley.

Cook, V. (2002) Background to the L2 users. In V. Cook (ed.) *Portraits of L2 Users* (pp. 1–28). Clevedon: Multilingual Matters.

Costley, T. (2008) 'You are beginning to sound like an academic': Finding and owning your academic voice. In C.P. Casanave and X. Li (eds) *Learning the Literacy Practices of Graduate School: Insiders' Reflections on Academic Enculturation* (pp. 74–87). Ann Arbor: University of Michigan Press.

Crabtree, R. and Weissberg, R. (2000) *ESL Students in the Public Speaking Classroom: A Guide for Teachers* (3rd edn). Boston, MA: Bedford/St. Martin's.

Cummins, J. (1979) Cognitive/academic language proficiency, linguistic interdependence, the optimal age question and some other matters. *Working Papers on Bilingualism* 19, 197–205.

Cummins, J. (2000) *Language, Power, and Pedagogy: Bilingual Children in the Crossfire.* Clevedon: Multilingual Matters.

Cummins, J., and Swain, M. (1986) *Bilingualism in Education: Aspects of Theory, Research, and Practice.* New York: Longman.

Curzan, A. and Adams, M. (2012) *How English Works: A Linguistic Introduction* (3rd edn). New York: Pearson Education.

Derwing, T.M. and Munro, M.J. (2005) Second language accent and pronunciation teaching: A research-based approach. *TESOL Quarterly* 39 (3), 379–398.

Derwing, T.M. and Munro, M.J. (2009) Putting accent in its place: Rethinking obstacles to communication. *Language Teaching* 42, 476–490.

Diebold, A.R., Jr. (1961) Incipient bilingualism. *Language* 37 (1), 97–112.

Elbow, P. (1993) Ranking, evaluating, and liking: Sorting out three forms of judgment. *College English* 55 (2), 187–206.

Ely, C.W. (1995) Tolerance of ambiguity and the teaching of ESL. In J.M. Reid (ed.) *Learning Styles in the ESL/EFL Classroom* (pp. 87–95). New York: Heinle and Heinle.

Emig, J. (1971) *The Composing Processes of Twelfth Graders.* NCTE Research Report 13. Urbana, Il: National Council of Teachers of English.

Eskey, D. and Grabe, W. (1988) Interactive models for second language reading: Perspectives on instruction. In P.L. Carrell, J. Devine and D. Eskey (eds) *Interactive Approaches to Second Language Reading* (pp. 223–238). Cambridge: Cambridge University Press.

Ferris, D.R. (2009) *Teaching College Writing to Diverse Student Populations.* Ann Arbor: University of Michigan Press.

Ferris, D. and Tagg, T. (1996) Academic oral communication needs of EAP learners: What subject-matter instructors actually require. *TESOL Quarterly* 30, 31–55.

Fishman, J.A., Cooper, R.L. and Newman, R.M. (1971) *Bilingualism in the Barrio*. Bloomington: Indiana University.

Flaitz, J. (ed.) (2003) *Understanding Your International Students: An Educational, Cultural, and Linguistic Guide*. Ann Arbor: University of Michigan Press.

Flaitz, J. (ed.) (2006) *Understanding Your Refugee and Immigrant Students: An Educational, Cultural and Linguistic Guide*. Ann Arbor: University of Michigan Press.

Flowerdew, J. (1994) Research of relevance to second language lecture comprehension – An overview. In J. Flowerdew (ed.) *Academic Listening: Research Perspectives* (pp. 7–30). New York: Cambridge University Press.

Freire, P. (1970) *Pedagogy of the Oppressed*. New York: Continuum.

Freire, P. and Macedo, D. (1987) *Literacy: Reading the Word and the World*. Cambridge, MA: Bergin & Garvey.

Friedman, T.L. (2006) *The World is Flat: A Brief History of the Twenty-First Century* (updated and expanded). New York: Farrar, Straus and Giroux.

García, O. (2009) *Bilingual Education in the 21st Century: A Global Perspective*. Chichester, West Sussex, UK: John Wiley & Sons.

Gebhard, J.G. (2010) *What Do International Students Think and Feel? Adapting to US College Life and Culture*. Ann Arbor: University of Michigan Press.

GlobalHigherEd (2011) International student mobility highlights in the OECD's Education at a Glance 2011. (2011, September 13). Online document: http://globalhighered. wordpress.com/2011/09/13/international-student-mobility-highlights-in-the-oecds-education-at-a-glance-2011/. Accessed 15.07.12.

Goffman, E. (1967) On face-work: An analysis of ritual elements in social interaction. In E. Goffman, *Interaction Ritual: Essays on Face-to-Face Behavior* (pp. 5–45). Chicago: Aldine.

Grabe, W. (2001) Reading-writing relations: Theoretical perspectives and instructional practices. In D. Belcher and A. Hirvela (eds) *Linking Literacies: Perspectives on L2 Reading-Writing Connections* (pp. 15–47). Ann Arbor: University of Michigan Press.

Graff, G. and Birkenstein, C. (2010) *They Say, I Say: The Moves that Matter in Academic Writing* (2nd edn). New York: W. W. Norton & Company.

Grellet, F. (1981) *Developing Reading Skills: A Practical Guide to Reading Comprehension Exercises*. Cambridge, England: Cambridge University Press.

Hafernik, J.J. (1991) Relationships among English writing experience, contrastive rhetoric, and English expository prose of L1 and L2 writers. Unpublished dissertation, University of San Francisco, San Francisco, CA.

Hafernik, J.J. and Wiant, F. (2007) Report on a survey of student writing issues at the University of San Francisco. Unpublished manuscript, College of Arts and Sciences, University of San Francisco: San Francisco, CA.

Hafernik, J.J., Messerschmitt, D.S. and Vandrick, S. (2002) *Ethical Issues for ESL Faculty: Social Justice in Practice*. Mahwah, NJ: Lawrence Erlbaum.

Harklau, L. (2000) From the 'good kids' to the 'worst': Representations of English language learners across educational settings. *TESOL Quarterly* 34, 35–67.

Harklau, L., Losey, K.M. and Siegal, M. (1999) Linguistically diverse students and college writing: What is equitable and appropriate? In L. Harklau, K.M. Losey and M. Siegal (eds) *Generation 1.5 Meets College Composition: Issues in the Teaching of Writing to US-Educated Learners of ESL* (pp. 1–14). Mahwah NJ: Lawrence Erlbaum.

Hashimoto, I.Y. (1991) *Thirteen Weeks: A Guide to Teaching College Writing.* Portsmouth, NH: Boynton/Cook.

Heath, S.B. (1983) *Ways with Words.* New York: Cambridge University Press.

Hinds, J. (1987) Reader versus writer responsibility: A new typology. In U. Connor and R.B. Kaplan (eds) *Writing Across Languages: Analysis of L2 Text* (pp. 141–152). Reading, MA: Addison-Wesley.

Hirasuna, D. (2005) *The Art of Gaman: Arts and Crafts from the Japanese American Internment Camps 1942 – 1946.* Berkeley, CA: Ten Speed Press.

Hirvela, A. (2004) *Connecting Reading and Writing in Second Language Writing Instruction.* Ann Arbor: University of Michigan Press.

Hu, H.C. (1944) The Chinese concept of face. *American Anthropologist* 46 (1), 45–64.

Huang, J. and Brown, K. (2009) Cultural factors affecting Chinese ESL students' academic learning. *Education* 129 (4), 643–653.

Institute of International Education (IIE). (2010). Opendoors (2010) 2010 fast facts. Online document: http://www.iie.org/en/research-and-publications/~/media/Files/Corporate/Open-Doors/Fast-Facts/Fast%20Facts%202010.ashx. Accessed 15.07.12.

Institute of International Education (IIE). (2011). Opendoors (2011) 2011 fast facts. Online document: http://www.iie.org/en/research-and-publications/~/media/Files/Corporate/Open-Doors/Fast-Facts/Fast%20Facts%202011.ashx. Accessed 15.07.12.

The International Center for Academic Integrity. Online at: www.academicintegrity.org/icai/home/php. Accessed 15.07.12.

Jacobus, L.A. (2010) Evaluating ideas: An introduction to critical reading. In L.A. Jacobus (ed.) *A World of Ideas: Essential Readings for College Writers* (8th edn) (pp. 1–11). Boston: Bedford/St. Martin's.

Jaschik, S. (2009, September 28) The Chinese are coming. *Inside Higher Ed.* Online at: http://www.insidehighered.com/news/2009/09/28/china. Accessed 15.07.12.

Johns, A.M. (1981) Necessary English: A faculty survey. *TESOL Quarterly* 15, 51–57.

Johns, A.M. (1991) Faculty assessment of ESL student literacy skills: Implications for writing assessment. In L. Hamp-Lyons (ed.) *Assessing Second Language Writing in Academic Contexts* (pp. 167–180). Norwood, NJ: Ablex Publishing.

Johns, A.M. (1999). Opening our doors: Applying socioliterate approaches (SA) to language minority classrooms. In L. Harklau, K.M. Losey and M. Siegal (eds) *Generation 1.5 Meets College Composition: Issues in the Teaching of Writing to US-Educated Learners of ESL* (pp. 159–171). Mahwah NJ: Lawrence Erlbaum.

Jule, A. (2004) Speaking in silence: A case study of a Canadian Punjai girl. In B. Norton and A. Pavlenko (eds) *Gender and English Language Learners* (pp. 69–78). Alexandria, VA: Teachers of English to Speakers of Other Languages, Inc.

Kadison, R. and DiGeronimo, T.F. (2004) *College of the Overwhelmed: The Campus Mental Health Crisis and What to Do About It.* San Francisco, CA: Jossey-Bass.

Kaplan, R.B. (1966) Cultural thought patterns in intercultural education. *Language Learning* 16 (1): 1–20.

Kaplan, R.B. (1987) Cultural thought patterns revisited. In U. Connor and R.B. Kaplan (eds) *Writing Across Languages: Analysis of L2 Text* (pp. 9–21). Reading, MA: Addison-Wesley.

Kern, R. (2000) Notions of literacy. In R. Kern (ed.) *Literacy and Language Teaching* (pp. 13–14). New York: Oxford University Press.

Kramsch, C. (1997) The privilege of the nonnative speaker. *PMLA* 112, 359–369.

Kutz, E., Groden, S.Q. and Zamel, V. (1993) *The Discovery of Competence: Teaching and Learning with Diverse Student Writers.* Portsmouth, NH: Boynton Cook.

Land, R.E. and Whitley, C. (2006) Evaluating second-language essays in regular composition classes: Toward a pluralistic US rhetoric. In P.K. Matsuda, M. Cox, J. Jordan and C. Ortmeire-Hooper (eds) *Second-Language Writing in the Composition Classroom: A Critical Sourcebook* (pp. 324–332). Boston: Bedford/St. Martin's. (Original work published 1989)

Lave, J. and Wenger, E. (1991) *Situated Learning: Legitimate Peripheral Participation* Cambridge, England: Cambridge University Press.

Leki, I. (1992) *Understanding ESL Writers: A Guide for Teachers*. Portsmouth, NH: Boynton/Cook.

Leki, I. and Carson, J. (1997) 'Completely Different Worlds': EAP and the writing experiences of ESL students in university courses. *TESOL Quarterly* 31, 39–70.

Li, X. and Casanave, C. (2008) Introduction. In C.P. Casanave and X. Li (eds) *Learning the Literacy Practices of Graduate School: Insiders' Reflections on Academic Enculturation* (pp. 1–11). Ann Arbor: University of Michigan Press.

Lippi-Green, R. (1997) *English with an Accent: Language Ideology and Discrimination in the United States*. New York: Routledge.

Liu, M. and Jackson, J. (2008) An exploration of Chinese EFL learners' unwillingness to communicate and foreign language anxiety. *The Modern Language Journal* 92 (1), 71–86.

Long, D.R. (1989) Second language listening comprehension: A schema-theoretic communication. *Modern Language Journal* 73, 32–40.

Matsuda, P.K. and Matsuda, A. (2009) The erasure of resident ESL writers. In M. Roberge, M. Siegal and L. Harklau (eds) *Generation 1.5 in College Composition: Teaching Academic Writing to US Educated Learners of ESL* (pp. 50–64). New York: Routledge.

McArthur, T. (ed.) and McArthur, F. (Managing ed.) (1992) *The Oxford Companion to the English Language*. Oxford: Oxford University Press.

McCabe, D. (2001) Cheating: Why students do it and how we can help them stop. *American Educator*, 25 (4), 38–43. (ERIC Documentation Reproduction Service No. EJ 642292).

McCabe, D.L., Treviño, L.K. and Butterfield, K.D. (2001) Cheating in academic institutions: A decade of research. *Ethics and Behavior* 11 (3), 219–232.

McCormick, K., Waller, G. and Flower, L. (1987) *Reading Texts: Reading, Responding, Writing*. Lexington, MA: D. C. Heath.

Mori, S. (2000) Addressing the mental health concerns of international students. *Journal of Counseling and Development* 78 (2), 137–144. (ERIC Document Reproduction Service No. EJ607751.)

Norton, B. (1997) Language, identity, and the ownership of English. *TESOL Quarterly* 31, 409–429.

Norton, B. (2000). *Identity and Language Learning: Gender, Ethnicity, and Educational Change*. Harlow, England: Longman.

Norton Peirce, B. (1995) Social identity, investment, and language learning. *TESOL Quarterly* 29, 9–31.

Ogbu, J. (1990) Cultural mode, identity, and literacy. In J.W. Stigler, R.A. Shweder and G. Herdt (eds) *Cultural Psychology: Essays on Comparative Human Development* (pp. 520–541). Cambridge: Cambridge University Press.

Olster, S.E. (1980) A survey of academic needs for advanced ESL. *TESOL Quarterly* 14, 489–502.

Panetta, C.G. (ed.) (2001) *Contrastive Rhetoric Revisited and Redefined*. Mahwah, NJ: Lawrence Erlbaum.

Pennycook, A. (1996) Borrowing others' words: Text, ownership, memory, and plagiarism. *TESOL Quarterly* 30, 201–230.

Pennycook, A., Chandrasoma, R. and Thomson, C. (2004) Beyond plagiarism: Transgressive and nontransgressive intertextuality. *Journal of Language, Identity and Education* 3 (3), 171–193.

Pinker, S. (1994) *The Language Instinct: How the Mind Creates Language.* New York: W. Morrow.

Purdue OWL. (2010, April 17) Higher order concerns (HOCs) and lower order concerns (LOCs) handout. Online at: http://owl.english.purdue.edu/owl/resource690/01/. Accessed 15.07.12.

Reid, J. (1993) Historical perspectives on writing and reading in the ESL classroom. In J.G. Carson and I. Leki (eds) *Reading in the Composition Classroom: Second Language Perspectives* (pp. 33–60). Boston: Heinle and Heinle.

Reid, J. (2006) 'Eye' learners and 'ear' learners: Identifying the language needs of international students and US resident writers. In P.K. Matsuda, M. Cox, J. Jordan and C. Ortmeier-Hooper (eds) *Second-Language Writing in the Composition Classroom: A Critical Sourcebook* (pp. 76–88). Boston: Bedford/St. Martin's. (Original work published 1998)

Roberge, M (2009) A teacher's perspective on generation 1.5. In M. Roberge, M. Siegal and L. Harklau (eds) *Generation 1.5 in College Composition: Teaching Academic Writing to US Educated Learners of ESL* (pp. 3–24). New York: Routledge.

Robinson, F.P. (1970) *Effective Study* (4th edn). New York: Harper and Row.

Rose, M. (1985) The language of exclusion: Writing instruction at the university. *College English* 47 (4) 341–359.

Rose, M. (2005) *Lives on the Boundary: A Moving Account of the Struggles and Achievements of America's Educationally Underprepared.* New York: Penguin Books. (Original work published 1989)

Russell, D. R. (2002) *Writing in the Academic Disciplines: A Curricular History* (2nd edn). Carbondale, IL: Southern Illinois University Press.

Sadker, M., and Sadker, D. (1994) *Failing at Fairness. How America's Schools Cheat Girls.* New York: Charles Scribner's Sons.

Scarcella, R.C. (1996) Secondary education in California and second language research. *CATESOL Journal* 9 (1), 129–152.

Scarcella, R.C. (2003) *Accelerating Academic English: A Focus on the English Learner.* Oakland: University of California.

Schmidt-Rinehart, B.C. (1994) The effects of topic familiarity on second language listening comprehension. *Modern Language Journal* 78, 79–89.

Sharber, E. (2009, March 19) Writing 'A' papers: High, middle, and low concerns. Online at: http://www.suite101.com/content/writing-a-papers-a103282. Accessed 15.07.12.

Shaughnessy, M. (1998) Diving in: An introduction to basic writing. In V. Zamel and R. Spack (eds) *Negotiating Academic Literacies: Teaching and Learning Across Languages and Cultures* (pp. 1–7). Mahwah, NJ: Lawrence Erlbaum. (Original work published 1976)

Shen, F. (1998) The classroom and the wider culture: Identity as a key to learning English composition. In V. Zamel and R. Spack (eds) *Negotiating Academic Literacies: Teaching and Learning Across Languages and Cultures* (pp. 123–133). Mahwah, NJ: Lawrence Erlbaum. (Original work published 1989)

Shin, H. and Bruno, R. (2003) *Language Use and Speaking Ability, 2000: Census 2000 Brief.* Summary report of the US Census Bureau. Washington, DC: U. S. Census Bureau. Online document: http://www.census.gov/prod/2003pubs/c2kbr-29.pdf. Accessed 15.07.12.

Shin, H. and Kominski, R.A. (2010) Language use in the United States 2007: American Community Survey Reports. US Department of Commerce, US Census Bureau.

Singhal, M. (2004) Academic writing and Generation 1.5: Pedagogical goals and instructional issues in the college composition classroom. *The Reading Matrix* 4 (3), 1–13. Online document: http://www.readingmatrix.com/articles/singhal/article2.pdf. Accessed 15.07.12.

Singleton, J. (1995) Gambaru: A Japanese cultural theory of learning. In J.J. Shields (ed.) *Japanese Schooling: Patterns of Socialization, Equality, and Political Control* (pp. 8–15). University Park, PA: Pennsylvania State University Press. (Original work published 1989)

Smith, A.H. (1894) *Chinese Characteristics*. New York: Fleming H. Revell.

Smith, F. (1988) Joining the literacy club. In *Joining the Literacy Club: Further Essays into Education* (pp. 1–16). Portsmouth, NH: Heinemann.

Soet, J. and Sevig, T. (2006) Mental health issues facing a diverse sample of college students: Results from the college student mental health survey. *NASPA Journal* 43 (3), 410–431.

Spack, R. (1997) The rhetorical construction of multilingual students. *TESOL Quarterly* 31, 765–774.

Spack, R. (2007) Exchanging feedback. In *Guidelines: A Cross-Cultural Reading/Writing Text* (3rd edn) (pp. 275–277). New York: Cambridge University Press.

Spender, D. (1980) *Man Made Language*. London: Routledge and Kegan-Paul.

Stanley, J. (2010) *The Rhetoric of Remediation: Negotiating Entitlement and Access to Higher Education.* Pittsburgh, PA: University of Pittsburgh Press.

StudentPOLL (2012) Definitive study of college-bound students in China (2012, February 27) *studentPoll* 1 (1), 1–15. Online at: http://www.artsci.com/StudentPOLL_China/v1n1/index.aspx. Accessed 15.07.12.

Swales, J.M. (1990) *Genre Analysis: English in Academic and Research Settings*. Cambridge, England: Cambridge University Press.

Turkle, S. (2004, January 30) How computers change the way we think. *The Chronicle of Higher Education* 50 (21) B26. Online document: http://web.mit.edu.sturkle/www/pdfsforstwebpage/Turkle_how_computers_change_way_we_think.pdf. Accessed 15.07.12.

United Nations Statistical Division (2011) Ethnocultural characteristics. Online at: http://unstats.un.org/unsd/demographic/sconcerns/popchar/default.htm. Accessed 15.07.12.

U.S. Department of Education. (n.d.) 'Family Educational Rights and Privacy Act (FERPA).' Online at: http://www2.ed.gov/policy/gen/guid/fpco/ferpa/index.html. Accessed 15.07.12.

Valdés, G. (2005) Bilingualism, heritage language learners, and SLA research: Opportunities lost or seized? *Modern Language Journal* 89 (3), 410–426.

Valdés, G. (2006) Bilingual minorities and language issues in writing: Toward profession-wide responses to a new challenge. In P.K. Matsuda, M. Cox, J. Jordan and C. Ortmeier-Hooper (eds) *Second-Language Writing in the Composition Classroom: A Critical Sourcebook* (pp. 31–70). Boston: Bedford St. Martin's. (Original work published 1992)

Valdés, G., MacSwan, J. and Alvarez, L. (2009) Deficits and differences: Perspectives on language and education. Online document: www.nationalacademics.org/../Peper—Valdés—McSwan—and—Alvarez.pdf. Accessed 22.10.11.

Vandrick, S. (1995) Privileged ESL university students. *TESOL Quarterly* 29, 375–381.

Vandrick, S. (2003) Language, culture, class, gender and class participation. Paper presented at TESOL International Convention. Vancouver, Canada. (ERIC Documentation Reproduction Service No. ED 473086). (Original work published 2000)

Vandrick, S. (2009) *Interrogating Privilege: Reflections of a Second Language Educator*. Ann Arbor: University of Michigan Press.

Vandrick, S. (2011) Students of the new global elite. *TESOL Quarterly* 45, 160–169.

Watters, E. (2010) *Crazy Like Us: The Globalization of the American Psyche*. New York: Free Press.

Wenger, E. (1998) *Communities of Practice: Learning, Meaning, and Identity*. Cambridge, England: Cambridge University Press.

Widdowson, H.G. (1994) The ownership of English. *TESOL Quarterly* 28, 377–389.

Wong, G. (2010, April 11) Research hurt by plagiarism, faked results. *The San Francisco Chronicle* p. A 12.

Yang, J. (2010) Lost in the puzzles. In M. Cox, J. Jordan, C. Ortmeier-Hooper and G.G. Schwartz (eds) *Reinventing Identities in Second Language Writing* (pp. 51–53). Urbana, Il: National Council of Teachers of English.

Yoon, C.K. (2009) *Naming Nature: The Clash Between Instinct and Science*. New York: W. W. Norton and Company.

Young, J.R. (2010, March 28) High-tech cheating abounds, and professors bear some blame. *The Chronicle of Higher Education*. Online at: http://chronicle.com/article/High-Tech-Cheating-on-Homework/64857. Accessed 15.07.12.

Zamel, V. (1994) Strangers in academia: The experiences of faculty and ESL students across the curriculum. *College Composition and Communication,* 46 (4), 506–521.

Zawacki, T.M. and Habib, A.S. (2010) 'Will our stories help teachers understand?' Multilingual students talk about identity, voice, and expectations across academic communities. In M. Cox, J. Jordan, C. Ortmeier-Hooper and G.G. Schwartz (eds) *Reinventing Identities in Second Language Writing* (pp. 54–74). Urbana, Il: National Council of Teachers of English.

Glossary

Accent – a pattern of pronunciation, generally associated with geographical locations, race or ethnicity, social class and/or age. According to McArthur and McArthur (1992: 9) in *The Oxford Companion to the English Language*, 'a way of speaking that indicates a person's origin and/or social class'. Examples include an Australian accent, an Indian accent, an upper class Bostonian accent and a working class London accent.

Accuracy – refers to 'correctness' or language usage that has few or only minor errors. It most often applies to grammar usage and/or pronunciation. The term is often contrasted with *fluency*. A language user may be accurate but not fluent or fluent but not accurate.

Articulation – In *The Oxford Companion to the English Language*, McArthur and McArthur (1992: 83) define its general usage as 'the act or process of speaking, especially so that every element can be clearly heard'.

Basic Interpersonal Communication Skills (BICS) – refers to conversational fluency or language skills needed in social situations, such as face-to-face communication. Children who develop normally acquire BICS in their native languages naturally without formal instruction, and individuals can usually acquire BICS in a natural setting as an L2 in a short period of time (Cummins, 1979; Cummins & Swain, 1986). Cummins (1979) makes a distinction between BICS and CALP. These two theories of BICS and Cognitive Academic Language Proficiency (CALP) have been criticized as failing to take social practices and power relations into account.

Bilingual – refers to an individual who knows or has some fluency with two languages as well as refers to texts in two languages (e.g. a bilingual book of poetry or dictionary). There is controversy over what degree of proficiency in the two languages is needed for an individual to be considered bilingual and controversy over the different types of bilinguals.

Bilingualism – the ability to use two languages with some competence. How one defines 'competence' in a language is complex and controversial. Different types of bilingualism have been posited.

Circumstantial bilingual – Valdés (2006: 37) defines this term as 'individuals who, because of their circumstances, find that they must learn another language in order to survive'. An example would be a Sudanese refugee in the United States who is learning or has learned English.

Code-switching – the process of going back and forth between languages within a conversation. Code-switching often occurs spontaneously among fluent bilingual speakers who share the same languages.

Cognitive Academic Language Proficiency (CALP) – refers to language needed in academic situations. CALP consists of academic language skills such as critical thinking skills, academic vocabulary, sophisticated grammar knowledge and strong reading/writing skills. CALP generally requires formal instruction and takes approximately seven years, under good conditions, to be acquired by native and non-native speakers. Some individuals, native and non-native speakers, never develop CALP sufficiently (Collier, 1987, 1989; Scarcella, 1996, 2003). Cummins's theories of BICS and CALP have been criticized as failing to take social practices and power relations into account.

Common Underlying Proficiency (CUP) and Transferability Theories – Jim Cummins (2000) theorizes that there is a Common Underlying Proficiency (CUP) among languages an individual knows which allows skills, ideas and concepts individuals learn in their first language (L1) to transfer to subsequent languages they learn. In other words, skills and concepts learned in one language do not have to be relearned in the second or third language. For example, if one learns how to read in a language, learning to read in a second language will be easier than if one is illiterate. The knowledge that written symbols represent sounds and words will transfer, although the symbols and the words will differ in the two languages.

Deficit models – models that compare individuals' language skills (or other skills) to an idealized standard and determine what the individuals 'lack', in which areas or skills they are deficit. It is a negative or subtractive way of looking at an individual's skills.

Dialect – Romaine (cited in García, 2009: 33) defines *dialect* as 'a subordinate variety of a language' in contrast to the standard, or more accepted, dialect of a language. In effect, this often means that the standard dialect is the norm or default, with other dialects seen as deviant. Dialects are generally based on geography (regional dialects), social class (social dialects) and/or ethnicity or race (ethnic dialects). Within a given community, a dialect may be accepted as the norm and not the larger society's standard dialect. (See the entry for *standard English*.)

Diction – has several definitions, one dealing with style, another with word choice, and yet another with speaking. In this book, we use the definition 'a way of speaking, usually assessed in prevailing standards of pronunciation and elocution: *clear/slovenly diction*' (McArthur & McArthur, 1992: 306).

Discourse – refers to both written and oral extended language. It is language that is connected and is more than one sentence.

Domain – an abstract construct proposed by Joshua Fishman *et al.* (1971). Romaine (cited in García, 2009: 47) explains that *domain* 'refers to a sphere of activity representing a combination of specific times, settings, and role relationships'. An example is a Spanish speaker in the United States who uses Spanish in the domains of family and friends whereas she uses English in the domains of school and work.

Dominant language – the language used by most people and generally used in official domains or environments such as school and government business.

Dynamic bilingualism – this term recognizes that bilingualism is not linear but is dynamic, 'drawing from the different contexts in which it develops and functions' (García, 2009: 53). Dynamic bilinguals easily move from one language to another, depending on the situation and what they want to accomplish. This movement from one language to another may not be conscious. For example, a Russian American fluent in English and Russian would use English at school and other US institutions but may use Russian at church, in her neighborhood and with her family. So, she can use English in the US Post Office and then walk across the street and use Russian to order lunch, or even turn around in line at the Post Office and speak to another person in Russian. The term dynamic bilingualism captures the linguistic complexity of today's global world.

'Ear' learners – a term coined by Reid (2006) to refer to individuals who learn a second (or third or fourth) language (i.e. English) through oral language, through listening to and speaking English, that is, through using the language orally. Individuals who speak a non-English language at home and learn English by living in an English-speaking country are often ear learners.

Elective bilingual – Valdés (2006: 37) defines these individuals as 'those who choose to become bilingual'. An example would be an English-speaking Canadian who learns and becomes fluent in Japanese.

Elocution – according to McArthur and McArthur (1992: 345) in *The Oxford Companion to the English Language*, 'the way in which someone speaks or reads aloud, especially in public (flawless elocution)'.

Emergent bilingual – a monolingual individual who is in the process of becoming bilingual through schooling and who keeps her home language. This is a positive term, showing an individual's potential instead of her deficit or lack of a language; whereas, terms such as English Language Learners (ELLs) or Limited English Proficient students (LEPs) (García, 2009: 177) emphasize the lack of language as a deficit.

Englishes – this term refers to the varieties of English around the world, making the point that there is no one 'standard' or 'correct' English; therefore, a plural form of the word, *Englishes*, is used or *World Englishes* or *Global Englishes*. Varieties of English include South African English, American English, British English, Singaporean English and Indian English.

English as a Foreign Language (EFL) – this term is generally used to describe English courses taught in a country where English is not generally spoken or used as an official language. Rather, it is taught as a foreign language, as Russian or Japanese is taught as a foreign language in the United States. It is also used to describe students who are studying English as a Foreign Language – *EFL* students.

English as a Second Language (ESL) – this term is generally used to describe English courses taught in a country where English is the dominant and/or official language. Individuals learn English as an additional language to their first or home language. It is also used to describe students who are studying English as a Second Language – *ESL students* – in a country where English is the commonly used language.

English for Academic Purposes (EAP) – this term is used to differentiate English for university and college studies, for academic studies, from general, conversational English.

English Language Learners (ELLs) – this term is applied to individuals learning English and second language users in K – 12 in the United States. It is generally used as an institutional label, and some argue (e.g. García, 2009) that it does not recognize students' ability with their home or first language.

English for Speakers of Other Languages (ESOL) – a term that is generally used to describe individuals who are studying English as a second or as an additional language (second, third, fourth, etc.). It is also used to describe classes for individuals learning English in an English speaking country or community.

English for Specific Purposes (ESP) – a term that describes English courses that are designed for specific disciplines, such as English for business, English for technology, English for biology and English for law.

'Eye' learners – a term coined by Reid (2006) to refer to individuals who learn a language (i.e. English) through books and classroom instruction, that is, by reading and writing. International students who study English formally in classrooms in their countries and in English-speaking countries tend to be eye learners.

Face – a term used in sociology, linguistics, applied linguistics and other disciplines. Early mention of face and face-work is attributed to Chinese scholars (e.g. Hu, 1944; Smith, 1894). Terms associated with face and face-work were further adapted and researched by Goffman (1967: 5) who defines *face* 'as the positive social value a person effectively claims for himself by the line others assume he has taken during a particular contact. Face is an image of self delineated in terms of approved social attributes – albeit an image that others may share, as when a person makes a good showing for his profession or religion by making a good showing for himself'. Face is important in sociolinguistics, especially in politeness theory. Common expressions in English are 'save face', and 'lose face'.

Family Educational Rights and Privacy Act (FERPA) – the Family Educational Rights and Privacy Act of 1974, commonly known as FERPA, is a federal law that protects the privacy of student education records for students who are 18 years old or older or students enrolled in postsecondary institutions. Students have specific, protected rights regarding the release of such records, and FERPA requires that institutions adhere strictly to these regulations (US Department of Education, n.d.).

First Language (L1) – this term refers to an individual's first language, sometimes called home language, mother tongue/language or native language. It is often used in contrast with L2, second language.

Fluency – a term to describe an individual's overall language skills, generally in speaking and writing, as natural sounding and seemingly done with ease and comfort. Less commonly, we speak of reading fluency as well as fluency in writing and speaking, the ease with which one reads and/or writes and/or speaks. This term is often contrasted with *accuracy*. A language user may be accurate but not fluent or fluent but not accurate.

Functional bilingual – a term coined by Diebold (1961) to denote individuals who have some competence with another language that allows them to perform meaningful, although not necessarily grammatically accurate, communication.

Generation 1.5 (Gen 1.5) – a term broadly used to include those students who are children of immigrants and those who perhaps immigrated at a young age and who typically speak their native language or L1 at home. All have gone to schools, for varying lengths of time, where English is the medium of instruction. In this book, we use the term in the broadest sense. An excellent and much more complete discussion of the derivation of the term 'Generation 1.5' and the controversies surrounding it can be found in Roberge (2009) 'A teacher's perspective on generation 1.5.'

Genre – type of texts that share certain linguistic and rhetorical characteristics. Examples include papers in computer science, novels, short stories, business case studies, biological science articles, poetry and essays.

Grammar – commonly refers to syntax or the way words form sentences and the rules of what constitutes good language usage. For example, an individual may say, 'I never learned English grammar', meaning that she doesn't think she knows the rules or how to identify different parts of a sentence (e.g. the subject, verb, direct object). Linguists use the term to apply to the entire system of a language, including phonology, morphology, syntax and semantics.

Heritage language – refers to the language of one's family or ancestors. It may be spoken at home, but individual family members may have limited or no facility with the language. Valdés (2005: 411) says that the term is 'used broadly to refer to nonsocietal and nonmajority languages spoken by groups often known as linguistic minorities'. For example, in the United States, a Vietnamese child growing up in a home where Vietnamese is seldom spoken or only by older relatives may grow up with no working facility with Vietnamese and in order to learn Vietnamese must take classes or have formal instruction. Her heritage language is Vietnamese.

Home language – the language that an individual uses at home with her family. This language may be different from the dominant language in the country, the one used officially.

Incipient bilingual – a term coined by Diebold (1961) to refer to individuals who are beginning to acquire competence in another language. Thus, it can be considered a minimalist definition according to García (2009: 44).

International English Language Testing System, Academic section (IELTS) – a standardized English test developed in the United Kingdom to measure test-takers' readiness for undergraduate and graduate academic studies in universities where English is the medium of instruction. The IELTS is mainly used in the United Kingdom and Southeast Asia. In recent years, it has become more widely used by universities in the United States for making admissions decisions.

International Phonetic Alphabet (IPA) – a transcription system, consisting of symbols and diacritics and widely used to indicate the pronunciation of words.

Kinesthetic learning (See tactile-kinesthetic learning) – a mode or style of learning that involves physical activity in contrast to listening or reading. Kinesthetic learners are sometimes called 'doers'. Examples include building a model, drawing a flow chart and role playing.

Language Minority Student – a student whose L1 or home language is not the standard language used at school. For example, a Spanish or Hmong speaker in an English-speaking country would be considered a language minority student. A language minority student is often multilingual and has command of the official language of the country.

Language transfer – the concept that literacy skills in one language (L1) transfer to a second/additional language (L2). Research suggests that the amount and type of transfer of literacy skills depends upon several factors, including similarities of the L1 and L2 languages and types of tasks.

Learner-centered classroom – describes a classroom where a variety of teaching styles are employed, and students are typically expected to be active participants. Activities are not always controlled by or revolve around the instructor. For example, in learner-centered classrooms not only are there lectures, but also students are expected to be involved in discussions, presentations, group work and so on.

Limited English Proficient Students (LEPs) – often used to refer to students who are studying English and have limited academic English skills. It is commonly used to describe students in K – 12 settings, and some argue (e.g. García, 2009) that it does not recognize students' ability with their home or first language.

Linguistic features – aspects of a language such as phonology, morphology, syntax (grammar) and semantics. The term is often used in contrast to content or rhetorical style.

Literacy – the ability to read and write. We use the term 'academic literacy' to refer to the ability to read and write academic texts.

Mainstream/mainstreamed – in describing classes, the distinction can be made between *mainstream* classes, for all students, and English as a Second Language (ESL) or English for Academic Purposes (EAP) classes, designed to assist language minority students improve their English academic language skills. Students may transition from EAP courses into *mainstream* courses, for example, a history or chemistry class. Students can then be described as *mainstreamed*.

Mechanics – a traditional definition is punctuation, spelling and formatting of papers. Today some prefer the term 'conventions of writing'.

Metalanguage – words and expressions used to talk about language and one's processes involved in language use. For example, an individual can talk about the recursive steps she takes when writing an assigned essay (e.g. brainstorming, writing an outline, making notes, writing a draft, revising and editing a draft and proofreading).

Morphology – the study of the system or word forms and how words are formed in a particular language.

Mother tongue or Mother language – defined by the United Nations as 'the language usually spoken in the individual's home in his or her early childhood' (United Nations, 2011).

Multilingual – refers to an individual who knows or has some fluency with a second language (or in many cases a third or fourth language), also refers to texts in more than one language (e.g. a multilingual book or dictionary). There is controversy over what degree of proficiency in a language is needed for an individual to be considered multilingual.

Multilingualism – the ability to use two, three or more languages with some competence. How one defines 'competence' in a language is complex and controversial.

Native English Speakers (NES) – traditionally this has been used to describe individuals whose first language (L1) is English (e.g. often monolingual English speakers in countries where English is the dominant and/or official language such as the United Kingdom, the United States, Australia, New Zealand). Today this definition of native speaker is challenged, especially as English has become a global language, more and more individuals speak English, and more and more varieties of English exist. Widdowson (1994) asks the question, 'Who owns English?' The term *Native English Speaker* (NES) is used in contrast to *Non-Native English Speaker (NNES)*. For convenience, in this book, we use this distinction, yet at the same time we acknowledge its limitations and erroneous assumptions.

Native language – the language that one learns as a child, generally in the home. Today there is much controversy over how to define a language as an individual's *native language*. For example, for an Indian child growing up speaking Indian English and Hindi, is English her native language as well as Hindi?

Non-Native English Speakers (NNES) – traditionally this term has been applied to individuals whose first language (L1) is not English. The distinction between native and non-native English speakers is becoming more blurred as the usage of English spreads around the world. For convenience, in this book, we use this distinction (NES and NNES); at the same time, we acknowledge its erroneous assumptions and limitations.

Nonstandard English – a term used to describe varieties of English or dialects that are commonly used as vernacular varieties but are not considered 'standard' and often not considered prestigious. These forms 'are often lumped together, with greater or less discrimination, as non-standard, substandard or deviant forms when judged against a dominant form that is taught in all schools and used by all major public and private institutions' (McArthur & McArthur, 1992: 980). Examples include African American Vernacular English (AAVE), Appalachian English and Cockney English. Nonstandard forms of English often do not have written forms.

Oracy – according to McArthur and McArthur (1992: 730) in *The Oxford Companion to the English Language,* 'the ability to express oneself (fluently) in speech'. This term is used in contrast to *literacy* (reading and writing skills).

Phonology – the study of the sound system and sound change of a particular language or language family.

Pragmatics – the study of how we communicate in language within a social context; social communication that goes beyond the meaning (semantics) and syntax (grammar) of expressions. For example, if an individual asks a stranger 'Do you have the time?' the individual wants to know what the time is. The individual is not looking for a

'Yes/No' answer, even though the structure of the question was 'Yes or No'. Additionally, pragmatics applies to knowing the appropriate language to use in particular social situations, for example, knowing that it is almost always inappropriate to ask certain questions in US culture such as 'How much money do you make?' or 'Why aren't you married?'

Pronunciation – the way a certain word is articulated. Dictionaries provide appropriate pronunciations of words with the use of a transcription system such as the International Phonetic Alphabet (IPA).

Rubric – a term with a variety of definitions. In education, the *Merriam-Webster* online dictionary defines it as 'a guide listing specific criteria for grading or scoring academic papers, projects, or tests'.

Second Language (L2) – a term used to describe a language learned in addition to an individual's first or native language (L1) and is used to contrast with an individual's L1. The term is applied to additional languages learned and is not limited to only applying to the second language one knows. In other words, it often refers simply to additional languages. L2 is also used to describe users and learners of languages one knows in addition to one's native or first language.

Semantics – the study of meaning in language, especially the meanings of words and sentences.

Standard English – a prestigious social dialect of English within an English-speaking country that is taught in schools and used by mainstream media and the government. McArthur and McArthur (1992: 982) in *The Oxford Companion to the English Language* state that 'In everyday usage, *standard* English is taken to be the variety most widely accepted and understood within an English-speaking country or throughout the English-speaking world. It is more or less free of regional, class, and other shibboleths, although the issues of a "standard accent" often causes trouble and tension.' McArthur and McArthur (1992: 982) observe that this 'widely used term . . . resists easy definition but is used as if most educated people nonetheless know precisely what it refers to'.

Suprasegmental – term used to describe linguistic features of prosody (rhythm, stress, tone and intonation of speech). Another term commonly used is *prosodic features*. Suprasegmentals or prosodic features are used in contrast to phonetic features, such as consonants and vowels. The use and comprehension of these linguistic features can facilitate or discourage effective communication. For example, in Standard American English rising intonation at the end of a sentence marks it as a question. Stress allows individuals to differentiate between *re'-cord,* the noun with the stress on the first syllable, and *re-cord',* the verb with the stress on the second syllable.

Surface error – a term applied to grammatical or pronunciation mistakes that are made in a text such as an error in subject-verb agreement (e.g. Tom like to study history of the British Empire.).

Syntax – 'systematic ways in which words combine to create well-formed phrases, clauses, and sentences' (Curzan & Adams, 2012: 509) or the rules for combining words into grammatical units.

Tactile-Kinesthetic Learning (See Kinesthetic Learning) – a mode of learning that involves physical activity in contrast to listening or reading. Examples include building a model, drawing a flow chart and role playing.

Target Language – refers to the language an individual is studying or learning; in translation it refers to the language the text is being translated into.

Teacher-centered classroom – describes a classroom in which the teacher dictates or controls all activities. Typically these are lecture-style classes in which students listen, take notes and give back the information they have gotten in the lectures on exams; student participation is limited or lacking completely.

Teachers of English to Speakers of Other Languages (TESOL) – the name of an international professional organization associated with the discipline of Teaching English as a Second Language (TESL). There are affiliates in the United States and abroad.

Teaching English as a Foreign Language (TEFL) – a term that refers to the discipline of teaching English in a country where English is not used officially and is taught as foreign languages such as German or Japanese are taught in the United States.

Teaching English as a Second Language (TESL) – a term that refers to the discipline of Teaching English to Speakers of Other Languages and is also used to refer to MA programs in the field. TESL is generally used for teaching English in countries where English is the common and official language.

Test of English as a Foreign Language (TOEFL) – a standardized test of academic English administered by the Educational Testing Service (ETS). There are two forms: the paper-based-test, pbtTOEFL, and the internet-based-test, ibtTOEFL. This test is widely administered and accepted by postsecondary institutions for admission purposes.

Threshold Hypothesis – a hypothesis that says that for language literacy skills to transfer from a first language (L1) to a second language (L2), a certain proficiency in the L2 is needed. In other words, there is a threshold of L2 proficiency that allows transfer of literacy skills. This language threshold is flexible, depending upon the task, text and reader; it is not a specific set of grammar rules or vocabulary.

Translanguaging – a term used by García (2009: 45) to describe 'the language practices of bilinguals from the perspective of the users themselves', that is, using the perspective of bilinguals themselves is in contrast to the more common practice of viewing language practices from the perspective of the language itself. García asserts that translanguaging goes beyond code-switching and that 'translanguagings are *multiple discursive practices* in which bilinguals engage in order to *make sense of their bilingual worlds*'. (Emphasis in the original text.).

Written accents – individual variations in voice, rhetorical style, and sentence construction in writing. It is analogous to individual accent in speaking.

Appendix: Sample Rubrics and Other Evaluation Tools

This appendix provides sample rubrics and other evaluation tools for a variety of academic tasks, including written assignments, oral presentations and discussions. We have organized our samples into three groups.

(1) Self-evaluation. Rubrics and guidelines for self-evaluation provide students with the opportunity to evaluate and reflect on their own work, whether it is the first or final copy of an essay or a speech or oral presentation, individual or group, given in class. Ideally, speeches and oral presentations are videotaped and students can view themselves and reflect on their performance.

(2) Peer evaluation. Evaluating others' work helps students learn to evaluate texts (spoken and written), get ideas about what works and doesn't work and become critical readers and listeners. By paying close attention to their peers' work, they acquire skills to help them critique their own work and gain a sense of how their work compares to their classmates'. We have found that students learn much from each other and also learn to appreciate what others bring to the class by being more aware of others' work.

(3) Faculty evaluation. Rubrics and other evaluation tools provide students and faculty with guidelines for evaluating work. By giving students evaluation tools ahead of time, faculty delineate what is important in the assignment and how it will be assessed. Such tools also provide a means for structured feedback.

In commenting on student work, whether drafts or finished products, we advocate commenting on positive aspects as well as areas for improvement. We believe that doing this helps students be more receptive to suggestions offered. The best rubrics and evaluation tools are course-specific and assignment-specific. Faculty can design rubrics that focus on what they think is most important and what they wish students to master. We hope the ones we have included here will serve as springboards for you creating your own.

Self-Evaluation of a Speech

Name: _____   Date: _____

View your speech online and answer the following questions:
(1) What are two things that you think you did well? Explain your answer.
(2) What are two areas that you think were weak and need improvement? Explain your answer.
(3) What can you do to improve your areas of weakness? What can you do differently for your next speech? Explain your answer.
(4) Describe how you felt while you were giving your presentation.
(5) What is one thing a classmate did well in his/her speech? Explain your answer.
(6) Were you an active listener when others were giving speeches? What did you do to support the speaker?

Self- Evaluation of Speech

Name: _____   Date: _____

(1) What are one or two things that you think you did well in your speech? Explain your answer.
(2) What are one or two things that were difficult for you in preparing and giving your speech? Explain your answer.
(3) How did you feel while you were giving your speech? How did you try to control your nervousness?
(4) On a scale of 1–5 with 5 being 'very good' and 1 being 'needs work', how would you rate yourself on each of the following components. Explain your answer.
> *Content of Presentation* (e.g. topic, thesis, interest, support, use of outside sources and appropriate documentation)
> *Organization:* (introduction, body, conclusion, transitions)
> *Delivery* (e.g. eye contact, demeanor, gestures, naturalness, volume and rate of speech, pronunciation, overall comprehensibility)
> *Language Effectiveness* (grammar control, vocabulary, comprehensibility)

(5) What is one thing a classmate did well? How can you use this example to help you improve?
(6) How would you compare your performance in this speech with your previous performances in this class? Explain your answer.

Self-Evaluation/Reflection for Essays

Name: _____   Date: _____

Use this rubric to guide you in working on drafts of each essay and in revising your essays. You may be asked to submit this reflection with each draft or bring it when you meet with your professor to discuss an essay.

Higher Order Concerns (HOCs) – Global Level

(1) Does the paper have a clear and concise thesis?
(2) Does the introduction contain a preview of the main arguments?
(3) Do the arguments contain sufficient evidence and reasoning to support the conclusions?
(4) Does the paper have an attention-getter and an effective conclusion?

Middle Order Concerns (MOCs) – Paragraph Level

(1) Does each paragraph have a topic sentence and support?
(2) Is the organizational pattern easy to follow? Do effective transitions lead naturally and logically from one point to the next?
(3) Do sentences reflect the old-new information pattern?
(4) Do sentences flow logically from one to the next?

Lower Order Concerns (LOCs) – Sentence Level

(1) Do all quotations, paraphrases and summaries have source citations?
(2) Do sentences contain specific and accurate verbs and avoid the over use of 'be' verbs and passive voice?
(3) Are adverbials used to vary the complexity of sentences and subordinate less important information?
(4) Are there errors in grammar, spelling or punctuation that need to be corrected?

Self- Reflection for Essays

Name: _____   Date: _____

Answer each question about your draft and submit it with your draft and/
or bring it to the conference with your professor.

(1) Is the paper in the correct format (e.g. double-spaced, a title, name and
    date on the first page, page numbers, running head, 1 inch margins)? If
    not, what did you forget?
(2) What is the thesis or focus of the paper? Where does this appear in your
    paper?
(3) What are three details that you include to support your thesis? Explain
    your answer.
(4) How do you tie your conclusion back to your introduction? Explain
    your answer.
(5) What was the easiest part of writing this essay? Explain your answer.
(6) What was the most difficult part of writing this essay? Explain your
    answer.
(7) What is one aspect of the paper that you would like me to pay close
    attention to and help you with? Explain your answer.

Self-Evaluation of Participation in a Group-led Discussion

Name: _____ Date: _____

Topic of Presentation: _____

(1) What are two things that you personally did well? What are two things that you as a group did well? Consider both the introductory comments and leading the discussion. Explain your answer.

(2) What adjustments were necessary to lead a discussion instead of simply making a speech? What adjustments to lead a discussion as part of a group? Explain your answer.

(3) What are two areas of your contribution that you feel need improvement?

(4) What challenges did you face when leading the discussion as a group? How did you deal with these challenges?

(5) What is one thing that another group did well? Explain your answer.

(6) What is one piece of advice that you would give someone who plans to lead a discussion, either by herself or in a group?

Add any other comments here.

Peer Speech Evaluation

(Each student has one evaluation form to complete for one speaker. In this way, each speaker has a peer evaluation and is asked at least one question.)

Speaker: _____   Date: _____

Peer Reviewer: _____

(1) What is one thing that the speaker did well? Explain your answer.
(2) What is one suggestion for improvement? Be specific and explain your answer.
(3) Write one or two questions about the content of the speech. Ask the speaker this question/these questions.
(4) Do you feel the speaker answered your questions adequately? Explain your answer.

Peer Essay Evaluation

Author: _____   Date: _____

Peer Reviewer: _____

Read your classmate's essay through completely and then answer the following questions. Remember that your purpose is to help your peer in revising her/his essay. Be honest in your answer and provide constructive comments. After completing your evaluation, discuss your comments and the essay with your classmate if time allows.

(1) Does the introduction make you interested in reading the rest of the paper? Explain your answer.
(2) Does the essay have a clear thesis or focus? What is it? Where is it in the essay?
(3) Does the author provide enough specifics and explanation to support her/his position/focus/thesis? If not, where would more details be useful?
(4) Are there any areas that you find difficult to understand? Where are they and why are they confusing? Explain your answer.
(5) Are there any areas that do not seem to relate to the focus/thesis/main point? Where are they? Explain your answer.
(6) What are one or two things that you think the author did well in this essay? What do you like about this essay? Explain your answer.
(7) What are one or two suggestions to help the author improve her/his draft?

Additional resource for peer evaluation

Spack, R. (2007) Exchanging feedback. In *Guidelines: A Cross-Cultural Reading/Writing Text* (3rd edn) (pp. 275–277). New York: Cambridge University Press.

Peer Evaluation of a Group Presentation

Presenters:_____

Topic:_____ Date:_____

Peer Evaluator: _____

Rate each of the following areas as *excellent* √+, *good* √ or *needs work* √-. Add comments to explain your rating and answer the questions below.

Area	Rating	Comments
Content (e.g. interest, appropriateness for audience and assignment, clear focus, good support and details, identified sources adequately)		
Organization (e.g. easy to follow, clear sections [introduction, body and conclusion], transitions, coherent)		
Delivery and Overall Communication (e.g. eye contact, appropriate volume and rate of speech, clarity of speech, comprehensibility, posture and body language, use of media and visual aids, all members well-prepared)		

(1) What is one thing that you learned from this presentation?
(2) What is one thing the group did well?
(3) What is one suggestion to help them improve future presentations?
(4) Additional comments

Faculty Rubric

Speech Evaluation and Comments

Speaker's Name: _____ **Date:** _____

Time: _____ (time allowed for speech = _____)

	Strong	Good	Needs Work	N/A	TOTAL for area
CONTENT and ORGANIZATION (Overall)	30	25	18		
a. Introduction	√+	√	√-		
b. Body	√+	√	√-		
c. Transitions/Connections	√+	√	√-		
d. Conclusion	√+	√	√-		
e. Audience awareness	√+	√	√-		
f. Accurate documentation of sources	√+	√	√-		
DELIVERY (Overall)	10	8	6		
a. Pace	√+	√	√-		
b. Volume	√+	√	√-		
c. Comprehensibility	√+	√	√-		
d. Pronunciation	√+	√	√-		
e. Posture	√+	√	√-		
f. Eye contact	√+	√	√-		
g. Gestures	√+	√	√-		
h. Use of note cards	√+	√	√-		
i. Use of PowerPoint or other aids	√+	√	√-		
j. Time within given range	√+	√	√-		
LANGUAGE EFFECTIVENESS (e.g. word choice, grammar, easy to understand)	10	8	6		
TOTALS					

General Comments and Suggestions:

Grading Scale: _____ /50   A: 45–50   B: 40–44

C: 35–39   D: 30–34   F: <12

Additional Resources for Evaluating Speeches

Morreale, S., Moore, M. Surges-Tatum, D. and Webster, L. (eds) (2007) *The Competent Speaker Speech Evaluation Form* (2nd edn). Washington, D.C.: National Communication Association (NCA). Online document: http://www.natcom.org/uploadedFiles/Teaching_and_Learning/Assessment_Resources/PDF-Competent_Speaker_Speech_Evaluation_Form_2ndEd.pdf. Accessed 26.07.12.

Speech Evaluation form directory. Online at: http://www.ratespeeches.com/a+speech-evaluation-form-directory. Accessed 26.07.12.

Faculty Rubric

Essay Evaluations and Comments

Higher Order Concerns (HOCs) – Global Level – 50%

1. Does the paper have a clear and concise thesis?	Yes	No
2. Does the introduction contain a preview of the main arguments?	Yes	No
3. Do the arguments contain sufficient evidence and reasoning to support the conclusions?	Yes	No
4. Does the paper have an attention-getter?	Yes	No
5. Does the paper have an effective conclusion?	Yes	No

Middle Order Concerns (MOCs) – Paragraph Level – 35%

1. Does each paragraph have a topic sentence and support?	Yes	No
2. Is the organizational pattern easy to follow? Do effective transitions lead naturally and logically from one point to the next?	Yes	No
3. Do sentences reflect the old-new information pattern?	Yes	No
4. Do sentences flow logically from one to the next?	Yes	No

Lower Order Concerns (LOCs) – Sentence Level – 15%

1. Do all quotations, paraphrases and summaries have source citations?	Yes	No
2. Do sentences contain specific and accurate verbs? Have you avoided the overuse of 'be' verbs and passive voice?	Yes	No
3. Are adverbials used to vary the complexity of sentences and subordinate less important information?	Yes	No
4. Are there errors in grammar, spelling or punctuation that need to be corrected?	Yes	No

Comments and Grade

Faculty Rubric for Essays/Written Assignments

(Faculty comment on the following broad categories of the written text. Percentages can be changed to fit specific assignments.)

Content (e.g. addresses the prompt/assignment, thesis, support, attention to audience, adequate in-text citations) 45%

Organization (e.g. transitions, coherence, clear organizational pattern {introduction, body, conclusion}) 35%

Language Effectiveness (e.g. grammatical and mechanical accuracy, clarity of sentences, fluency, sentence variety) 10%

Formatting (e.g. appropriate documentation, double-spaced, title, references) 10%

Grade: _____

Faculty Comments

Rubric for Essay #3: A Response to a Text

Name: **Date final submitted to *Turnitin*:**

	Strong	Adequate	Needs Work	Item(s) Missing
1. The **introductory paragraph** has: a. an interesting, relevant 'hook' and context/background;	2	1	0	0
b. a thesis statement with opinion and controlling ideas; and	3	2	1	0
c. the controlling ideas are parallel.	1	0	0	0
2. The **body paragraphs**: a. have topic sentences and relevant details and examples;	3	2	1	0
b. follow the order of the thesis statement;	1	0	0	0
c. use quotes and paraphrases from texts to support main ideas; and	3	2	1	0
d. introduce quotes and paraphrases with a variety of reporting verbs.	4	3	2	0
3. The **concluding paragraph** restates the thesis with different words and/or structure.	2	1	1	0
4. **All 'borrowed language'** is correctly quoted and cited.	4	3	2	0
5. Quotes are correctly **punctuated** (quotation marks, commas, periods).	4	3	2	0
6. **Slang and informal language** are avoided.	2	1	0	0
7. **Transitions** (FANBOYS, for example, however, etc.) are correctly used and punctuated.	3	2	1	0
8. **Subordinators** (because, when, as, if, etc.) are correctly used and punctuated.	3	2	1	0
9. **Feedback** is followed, the paper is **spellchecked**, and **MLA formatting** is used.	3	2	1	0
10. Essay is **appropriate length**.	2	1	0	0
subtotals				
Deductions: Late submission of draft or final copy. (-1 to -4)				
Score and grade A: 37–40 C: 29–32 F: <27 B: 33–36 D: 27–28	_____ / 40			

Developed by Christy Newman

Faculty Comments

Essay Three: Homework Grade: _____   **Essay Three Grade:** _____

Essay Three: Argument
First Draft
Completeness – minimum 750 words (5 pts)
Fulfills the purpose of the assignment (5 pts)   _____
MLA paper format (5 pts)   _____
Stapled (5 pts)   _____
Reviewed by instructor (5 pts)   _____
Introductory paragraph (5 pts)   _____
Total (30 pts):   _____

Second Draft
Completeness – minimum 750 words (5 pts)
Clearly revised for global revisions (5 pts)   _____
MLA paper format (5 pts)   _____
Stapled (5 pts)   _____
Reviewed by instructor (5 pts)   _____
Total (25 pts):   _____

Global Revision Questionnaire (10 pts)   _____
Peer Analysis (10 pts)   _____
Total (20 pts)

Homework Total:

Final Draft:

Introduction (10 pts) [Effectively orients the reader – that is, introduces the subject/sets up the debate, using one of the class-discussed introductory strategies; provides a clear argumentative thesis]

Development (10 pts) [Sufficient support for ideas, using at least 3 argumentative techniques – 3 appeals (ethos, logos, pathos), counter-argument, style]

Organization (10 pts) [Paragraph order, cohesion, coherence, adequate transitions between and within paragraphs, topic sentences]

Punctuation/Mechanics/Grammar/Style (10 pts)

MLA in-text and end-of-text documentation (10 pts)

Essay Total:
Developed by Cynthia Schultes

Faculty Rubric – Group Persuasive Speech (Debate) Evaluation Form

Group 1 (For) _____

References (20 pts) _____
Visual aids (10 pts) _____
Attention getter (5 pts) _____
Organization/Teamwork (30 pts) _____
Delivery (20 pts) _____
Closing (10 pts) _____
Time (5 pts) _____
Total (100 pts) _____   **Comments:**

Group 1 (Against)_____

References (20 pts) _____
Visual aids (10 pts) _____
Attention getter (5 pts) _____
Organization/Teamwork (30 pts) _____
Delivery (20 pts) _____
Closing (10 pts) _____
Time (5 pts) _____
Total (100 pts) _____   **Comments:**

Developed by Marc Martin

Index